GOD'S EYE VIEW
WORKBOOK

GOD'S EYE VIEW
WORKBOOK

WORSHIPING YOUR WAY
TO A HIGHER PERSPECTIVE

TOMMY TENNEY

THOMAS NELSON PUBLISHERS®
Nashville

A Division of Thomas Nelson, Inc.
www.ThomasNelson.com

Printed in the United States of America

02 03 04 05 06 VG 6 5 4 3 2 1

CONTENTS

INTRODUCTION

Millions of people from around the world learned about the personal and passionate pursuit of God's presence through *The God Chasers*. Then they caught a glimpse of the corporate pursuit of God's presence in *God's Favorite House*. Later, we discovered how to lengthen the moment of our encounter with His presence in *The God Catchers*. Now *God's Eye View* presents us with a backstage pass, a heavenly passport into God's presence.

When asked to describe this new book, I often reply, "If *The God Chasers* put you on your face, then *God's Eye View* will put you in the clouds." This is the fourth major book I've written on accessing the presence of God. I am blessed and amazed by the hunger these books have ignited in the hearts of so many, and I am also deeply aware of the identity of the true author behind these books and others I've written.

It all began when I literally observed the earthly scene from *God's Eye View* as I was lifted on the wings of intense worship. The divine encounter permanently changed my perspective of His presence and its relationship to the Christian life. If any credit or praise is offered because of the impact these books have made in the lives of readers, I joyfully pass it on to the Lord Jesus Christ, who alone is worthy of praise.

Time and again, I am asked by people from many cultures if I have prepared any study materials on the content of my books. It is with this need in mind that I prepared the *God's Eye View Workbook.* Remember that this workbook is not His presence; it is not your destination but a road map to a destination. You study it just as you might study a road map before starting your car to begin a journey.

My desire is that more and more God Chasers follow the pattern of the New Testament Jewish believers of Berea, who were careful to check everything Paul said against the Scriptures to see if they were true:

> Then the brethren immediately sent Paul and Silas away by night to *Berea.* When they arrived, they went into the synagogue of the Jews. These were more fair-minded than those in Thessalonica, in that they received the word with all readiness, and searched the Scriptures daily *to find out whether these things were so.* (Acts 17:10–11, emphasis added)

The most important thing you can do when God touches your life through a sermon, message, or book such as *God's Eye View,* is to compare and confirm everything stated with the unchanging truths of the Holy Scriptures to assure yourself that the things said and written are true.

Each chapter of the *God's Eye View Workbook* is designed to provoke thought and encourage personal application of the Bible truths and principles contained in *God's Eye View.* If you are like me, you have neither the time nor the interest to do mere busywork under the guise of Bible study. Each exercise in these chapters was written with a very specific purpose in mind.

Sections titled *Erroneous Assumptions, Presumptions, and Misaligned Paradigms,* for instance, are designed to expose and encourage careful examination of specific nonbiblical paradigms, practices, or thought patterns that are accepted in many modern churches, despite their extrabiblical origins.

Expect to provide your opinion about the way your life, worship, service, and witness are affected by the clash between conflicting attitudes or mind-sets any time you see the heading *What Do You Think?*

The purpose driving this project is simple and direct: I pray that your passionate worship of God will lift you to heavenly realms in His presence and impart to you *God's Eye View* of His purposes and your personal destiny in Him.

Remember that the *God's Eye View Workbook* is a tool to help you draw closer to Him and grow deeper in your Christian faith. It is *not* a race, so your goal should not be to "rush to the finish line first." Spread your wings in praise and worship and "mount up with wings like an eagle." Allow worship to lift you higher for a *God's Eye View* of things as, cheek to cheek, you seek the face of God and, suddenly, things look different.

TOMMY TENNEY

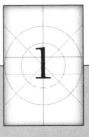

PICK ME UP, DADDY!

"I CAN'T SEE FROM DOWN HERE"

God never intended to limit your vision to the low point of view. He always intended for you to view things from the highest perspective, and worship is His way of lifting us above the mundane press of our enclosed space to see things from His point of view. (p. 3)

Your journey with Jesus may often lead you in some very unexpected directions. On the day I received the revelation that inspired this book, He walked into a crowded elevator with my daughter and me to show me how we see things differently.

ERRONEOUS ASSUMPTIONS, PRESUMPTIONS, AND MISALIGNED PARADIGMS

Some people question whether it is possible or even "proper" to wonder how things look from God's point of view. Your view on this question may explain a great deal about your life and your relationship with God. Have *you* ever wondered how things look from God's eye view?

❑   No, it is wrong for mere human beings to "wonder" how things look from God's point of view.

❑   No, it never occurred to me to ask the question.

❑   Only sometimes, when my own views aren't working.

❑   Yes. It helps me make decisions, renew my mind, and change my behavior in line with God's Word.

Each of these answers reveals basic assumptions or paradigms you have about God and the way He deals with people like you and me. It is normal and acceptable to make assumptions or hypotheses about God as long as *they are based upon consistent evidence from His Word.* The problems come when we don't have any evidence, or when we gather and apply it inconsistently as it pleases us or to justify our personal views. Ask yourself:

1. Which of my assumptions about God are *not* based upon consistent biblical evidence?

2. What am I going to do about my erroneous or unsupported assumptions?

3. How do you reconcile the Old Testament statement "For My thoughts are not your thoughts"[1] with the New Testament passage that says, "'*Who can know what the Lord is thinking? Who can give him counsel?*' But we can understand these things, *for we have the mind of Christ*"[2]?

FILLING THE VOID

Worship is the _____ of stretching your arms to the heavens in the
_____ ____ of _____ and desperation. It is the way
_____ creatures _____ the _____ of their heavenly Creator.
When you _____, it is as if you look at your _____ _____ and
say, "I don't like the way things look down here, Daddy. Would You ____ __ __?
I want to see things from ____ _____ of ____." (p. 2)

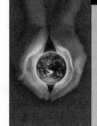

REMEMBER THIS

If all of this seems overly complicated, return to the mental picture of a
nervous three-year-old with his arms lifted straight toward his daddy's
face: *this is the posture of worship.* (p. 3)

WHAT DO YOU THINK?

Ever since the human race began its first "build-a-stairway-to-heaven-your-self" project in the city of Babel, people have been trying to "do it them-selves" in every area of life. Are you trying to do some things God never intended for you to do on your own?

No matter how educated, self-motivated, successful, or independent you become as an adult, the journey of life inevitably will bring you to your knees in some way. You are like a three-year-old in a crowded elevator. The expanse of jostling knees and purses offers no clues to your future and provides no hope for a better view.

When that happens, you need more than an attitude adjustment; you need an *altitude adjustment*. You need to view circumstances as your heavenly Father sees them. (p. 4)

1. Have you ever had that "little person in a big person's elevator" feeling? What caused it and what did you do about it?

2. Authoritative voices in the popular culture and on television talk shows often recommend that adults treat the "three-year-old" syndrome with various "self-empowerment" and "attitude adjustment" techniques. Does this match the counsel in God's Word?

3. Whose power and attitude do you need the most at any given moment?

TAKE IT
PERSONALLY!

Worship permits you to see things as your heavenly Father sees them. It lifts you from the pit of humanity's problems to a higher and purer perspective from the seat of Divinity. The power of a higher perspective is accessed through worship. Worship will lift your spirit. Worship will change your destiny. Worship will rearrange your future. (p. 4)

MORE ERRONEOUS ASSUMPTIONS, PRESUMPTIONS, AND MISALIGNED PARADIGMS

Many of us hold erroneous assumptions about Satan that may hamper our effectiveness in the kingdom. Sometimes we build him up larger than he really is, and at other times we underestimate his hatred for us and God's purposes. Have you ever wondered about what *he* fears, dreads, or hopes will happen in the lives of Christians?

Satan is intimidated by anyone who isn't afraid to bruise his heel in the process of crushing Satan's serpentlike head. Yes, a heel bruise may make you limp, but a crushed head is fatal. He cringes over the possibility that you may discover your God is bigger than every demonic image or scheme he conjures up.

He fears the day you shed your limited concepts of God and allow worship to elevate your perspective. The enemy dreads the moment worship causes you to lift your hands up to the One he fears above all others. He knows the game is up the moment your heavenly Father lifts your perspective into the heavenlies for a new view of life's low-level landscapes. (p. 5)

1. Do you expect to go through life as a Christian without ever "bruising your heel" in scuffles against the enemy's schemes and devices? Explain your answer.

2. In what practical ways is your God "bigger than Satan" in your life?

3. When everything seems to go wrong in your life, do you lift your
   fist in disgust or raise your arms in the sweet surrender of worship?

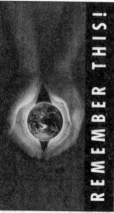

REMEMBER THIS!

Satan fears the heel-bruising, head-crushing anointing to worship.
He has always tried to snuff out the fire of anointing, kill the
prophets, or discredit the messenger—anything to postpone his
preappointed destruction.

    The same worship that elevates you depresses demons. In
other words, what lifts you up forces Satan down. "Down" is the
ultimate forwarding address for Lucifer. (p. 6)

FILLING THE VOID

Spread your wings and fly on the _____ of _____. Understand the power of
_____ and discover what _____ will do. Worship possesses the
_____ to make the _____ you _____ seem _____ while
_____ other things. (p. 7)

TAKE IT
PERSONALLY!

If you don't like the way things look "down here," then *change your perspective.* God has given you the key—*worship* can take you to a completely different understanding and lift you to a new plane of reality. (p. 7)

WHAT DO YOU THINK?

Worship is heaven's tool of choice for readjusting skewed human perspectives. Worship possesses a supernatural ability to correct our spiritual vision problems and bring everything into divine focus. If Daddy isn't worried, why should I feel discouraged? (p. 8)

1. How do you change your perspective in the face of potential discouragement or bitterness over broken dreams?

2. Do you take your "faith cue" from your circumstances or from your heavenly Father's attitude and His eternal Word?

REMEMBER THIS!

Size, mass, and height all seem to depend on the height of your vantage point. The elevation of your observation site determines whether you say you are looking "up there" or "down there." (p. 9)

MORE ERRONEOUS ASSUMPTIONS, PRESUMPTIONS, AND MISALIGNED PARADIGMS

Sometimes I am afraid that God is whispering to our deafened ears, *You might as well close down this service.* Why? We act as if we don't really want any interruptions from our Divine Customer. We are too busy blessing and congratulating one another on our funny stories, shallow sermons, gifted solos, and splendid choir renditions. We are irritated by every interruption . . . (p. 12)

This quote includes three broad categories of reasons God might advise us to close down our "worship" services. Either list them or come up with your own. Either way, you have to reconsider the way you "do" worship in your local church:

1.

2.

3.

TAKE IT
PERSONALLY!

This thing we call church isn't centered on your need to get a blessing or a divine tip. It seems the only way to be blessed is to wait on Him. *We wait* on God by *worshiping Him.* (p. 13)

WHAT DO YOU THINK?

I fear that we prostitute the presence of God by asking others to worship their way into a revelation and then share it with us. But if you *wait* on Him, if you personally pay the price to worship your way into His presence, He will lift you in His arms and give you a view you'll never forget. (p. 15)

What do you think (in your own words)?

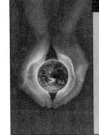

REMEMBER THIS!

Our capacity to give Him worship is not nearly as great as His capacity to receive it. We just need to keep piling it on. Corporate worship isn't really about how many people come to a meeting; it is about how much of Him shows up. (p. 16)

TAKE IT
PERSONALLY!

At some point your hunger for Him should show up in your willingness to worship and wait on Him. (p. 16)

FILLING THE VOID

____ appeared at a _____ attended by only 120 of the ____ _____ invited to attend it early in the first century. Those determined people _____ and _____ until __ _____ up, so He set their _____ on _____, spit them out _____ the _____ late in the morning, and _____ them into a ____-member bonfire _____ by lunchtime.[3] (p. 17)

WHAT DO YOU THINK?

Perhaps you've noticed that the concept of "waiting" appears very often throughout the Bible. Have you ever wondered why God's Word talks about "waiting" so much?

Are you ready to have church now? I can't prove this, but this is the way I think: *Could it be that the importance of spiritual events may have a direct correlation with the investment and measure of the wait involved?* (p. 17)

1. Salvation comes by faith through Jesus Christ, who paid the price with His own life. *After salvation* comes the command to all, "Let him deny himself, and take up his cross daily, and follow Me."[4] Does this sound like a "costly" or a "cheap" investment?

2. What kind of investment or "wait" do you make to welcome His presence in your life and in your worship gatherings?

MORE ERRONEOUS ASSUMPTIONS, PRESUMPTIONS, AND MISALIGNED PARADIGMS

It has been said that a Christian's life is the only Bible available to most of the people outside the kingdom. If that is true, then we may have grossly rewritten God's Word to say to the careful observer, "Teach me, Lord, how to hurry up because it's almost concession time. It's only twenty-five minutes till the holy noon hour, and we still have to pack in two solos, take up an offering, announce the coffee cake fund-raiser, and beat First Church to the restaurant." (p. 18)

1. What do people think of God when they read the "chapter and verse" of your life in your local community?

2. What do you need to do to make your personal "living version" of the Bible truer to the original?

WHAT DO YOU THINK?

Our appetite for fast food, speedy service, and rapid religion is clogging our arteries. It raises our blood pressure and puts more distance between us and the One who said, "Be still, and know that I am God."[5] It's time to raise our voices (and perhaps our hands) and worship. "Pick me up, Father." (p. 19)

What do you think (in your own words)?

REMEMBER THIS!

Counterfeit revival is a man-made product. Genuine revival—the type that permanently changes human lives and affects entire communities, nations, and generations—is costly and therefore rare. God entrusts divine visitation and heavenly habitation only with people who would die to taste His life. (p. 19)

MORE ERRONEOUS ASSUMPTIONS, PRESUMPTIONS, AND MISALIGNED PARADIGMS

Some of us believe that if our faith is strong enough, then we won't have any tests or defeats in our Christian walk. Others (whom God loves just as much) live as if everything in life is a test and difficulty. Most of us can be found somewhere between these two opinions. I decided to stir up the pot of opinion in *God's Eye View* just to make us think a little deeper about the role of "tests" in the development of our testimonies:

Everyone wants a dynamic testimony, but no one wants to experience the dynamic *test* it takes to produce such a testimony. If you really want an encounter with Divinity, make sure you are willing to move your humanity into the proper position for that encounter. I'm talking about your ability and willingness to worship your way into His presence and then wait—as if in divine pregnancy—for an outbreak of God's presence. Once you say, "Okay, God," then you had better buckle your seatbelt. (p. 20)

1. The idea that Christians should have no tests in life is backed up by people whose personal testimony begins and ends with the day they received Jesus Christ as LORD and Savior. Describe how God has helped or delivered you since the day you came to Him.

2. If you believe life is an unending test and drudgery, then it is *assumed* that salvation in Jesus makes very little difference for you *in this life*. How can the Cross affect what happens in the spiritual realm and leave the natural realm devoid of divine intervention?

3. Describe how the following Scripture passage applies to your daily life. How is this a picture of the way God transforms us *through* or *in spite of* tests in life, and makes it dramatically evident to those around us?

He died for all, that those who live *should live no longer for themselves, but for Him* who died for them and rose again. Therefore, from now on, *we regard no one according to the flesh.* Even though we have known Christ according to the flesh, yet now we know Him thus no longer. Therefore, if anyone is in Christ, *he is a new creation; old things have passed away; behold, all things have become new.*[6]

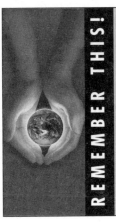

REMEMBER THIS!

The process of waiting on God in persistent and passionate worship almost seems like work to us; but Satan sees it in far more dramatic terms. He *fears* and *dreads* the day God's people set their hearts to pray and worship the Most High God. That should explain why Beelzebub, the lord of the flies, always seems to show up when we begin to worship God more than usual. (p. 21)

FILLING THE VOID

The _____ is at ease knowing that we love _____ _____ and _____ equations so much. He doesn't even get especially upset when we begin to sing _____ _____ by gifted psalmists and _____ leaders—as long as we _____ _____ according to some _____ _____ or church evangelism _____. It's when _____ is mixed into the recipe that the _____ of _____ begins to fear the _____! (p. 21)

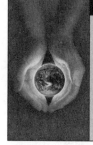

REMEMBER THIS!

God loves us too much to allow us to live in presumption. That is why He "moves the door" on us. He refuses to allow His relationship with us to deteriorate into ritual. We crave ritual, but God longs for relationship. (pp. 21–22)

NOTES

NOTES

THE VIRTUE OF ZERO

LESS IS BETTER AND NOTHING IS BEST

The Bible tells us it takes a fool to say there is no God.[1] Perhaps it takes an even bigger fool to say there is a God and then act as if His help isn't needed. This should explain why most of the confrontation in Jesus' ministry involved religious people and trained but tainted religious bureaucrats who should have known better. (p. 24)

In more ways than we want to admit, the culture of God's kingdom runs counter to the popular culture of North America and most Western nations. One is based totally on the character, will, and purposes of God; the other focuses on secular and human values—often in direct opposition to God's Word.

You and I are "caught" in the middle between the Rock and the hard place of compromise. There is no better place to discover the virtue of zero than in the "middle place" where less is better and nothing is best.

ERRONEOUS ASSUMPTIONS, PRESUMPTIONS, AND MISALIGNED PARADIGMS

Tryouts for God's team are radically different from those for any other team in the universe. To begin with, no one is "good enough." We join out of our necessity to *lean* instead of our ability to *leap*. We are rated for our capacity to go *low* instead of our ability to go *high*. The highest positions on the God squad go to the least among us, and the places of great honor go to those who come to Him with the emptiest and hungriest hearts. This is the virtue of zero, and one of the secrets to attaining a God's eye view of life. (p. 23)

This passage from *God's Eye View* challenges many of the most cherished assumptions, presumptions, and paradigms of our modern society. Are you prepared for heart surgery?

1. Are you prepared to spend your life going "low" before Him instead of climbing "high" before men? (Describe ways this statement might apply to your life.)

2. Do you define great honor in terms of accomplishments and fame or in terms of emptiness and hunger for God? (What are the implications of your answer?)

WHAT DO YOU THINK?

The unpleasant truth is that much of the work of character development takes place near what we might call our personal *ground zero*. Scientists coined this term around 1946 to describe the point at which a nuclear explosion occurs. I'm using the term to refer to "the center or origin of rapid, intense, or violent activity or change; the very beginning: square one."[2] More recently this term was used to refer to the place of devastation left after the tragedy of the Twin Towers of the World Trade Center in New York City.[3] (p. 24)

REMEMBER THIS!

If you take credit for the provision of Deity, you may stop His provision in your life and see your bank account drop and your blood pressure rise. The moment you take the glory for yourself, everything follows you—in the wrong direction. (p. 25)

WHAT DO YOU THINK?

Our God loves the challenge of a zero balance. To us, they look null and void, but from His viewpoint they represent pregnant emptiness and untapped potential waiting for divine touch. (p. 26)

What about the "zero places" in *your* life? Describe them and comment on how God might view them and use them for His glory.

FILLING THE VOID

They were ____ _____, but some _____ would add "and that was _____ __." Their résumés taken together didn't ___ ___ to _____ in the minds of the _____ _____—but in God's purposes, that _____ _____ had all of the characteristics of His _____ _____ place. (p. 27)

WHAT DO YOU THINK?

God prefers to invest His glory in the impossible and improbable because it is always clear that Deity did it, not the hand of flesh. Ego appears when humanity takes front stage to claim the glory—it tends to go to our heads and pollute our spirits. Evil walks through the door that ego opens. (p. 27)

1. What do you think about this quote from *God's Eye View*?

2. What kind of investment are you? Is your life filled with the flat faithless landscape of the entirely predictable and the totally possible, or is it marked by landmarks of impossibility and mountains of obstacles that dwarf your own strengths and resources? (Please explain your answer in detail.)

3. Where is God's presence and faithfulness most clearly present or most urgently needed in your life?

FILLING THE VOID

When He calls us to _____ the _____ and accomplish the _____, He receives ____ of the _____. When the _____ becomes _____ and the _____ becomes ____ through the hand of Divinity, _____ must humbly admit, "____ did that." (p. 28)

TAKE IT
PERSONALLY!

If all you have to sow into God's ground is your weakness, your pitiful praise, or a tiny seed of faith, then your "zero" may be enough to birth a miracle in your life! God is waiting for us to run to Him when we wake up at ground zero. One of the greatest opportunities we have to give Him glory is *the day we discover we are helpless, hopeless, and worthless unless He shows up.* (pp. 28–29)

MORE ERRONEOUS ASSUMPTIONS, PRESUMPTIONS, AND MISALIGNED PARADIGMS

The man with one talent [in the "parable of the talents"] thought he knew enough about God (symbolized by the king) to say He was constantly reaping where He had not sown, but he didn't have God's perspective on the situation.

God had sown the breath of life in the man. He sowed the talent of gold in the man's safekeeping, and He sowed the faith of Deity into the flesh of humanity. God *never* truly reaps where He has not sown—everything we are, everything we have, and all that we ever hope to be or accomplish comes ultimately from Him. (p. 30)

Presumption is one of the greatest dangers you will face in this life. It shows up in ways that totally escape our "spiritual radar" day after day. For instance:

1. How many times each day do you stop to thank God for the breath He gives you moment by moment? Do you talk about tomorrow and next year as if they are guaranteed to you by God? (See James 4:13–17.)

2. How will your perspective change if you begin to think of your life as a "field" into which God has sown His ability, purpose, and glory?

WHAT DO YOU THINK?

Nothing is far more significant to God than *something*. When you reach the point where you can't take any credit, *you are standing in fertile ground for glory*. This is the great significance of "nothing."

Now for a shocking revelation: your vision, your ministry, and your circumstances *must require a miracle,* or God literally will diminish your resources until He gets you on miracle territory. (p. 31)

1. Are we taking this point too far, or should we take it even further? It all depends on how you define a *miracle*. For most of us, God calls us to do the "mundane" supernaturally. If you feel called to feed and clothe the poor, will you do it to the extent that your own strength and resources last, or will you choose to lean on God for supernatural provision and supernatural results?

2. If you are called to adopt an unwanted child, will you do it in your own compassion or through the anointing and provision of God?

3. Does the principle change with the call? Is the process the same whether God asks you to raise your children to serve Him or if He asks you to move to Singapore and devote your life to training indigenous ministers throughout the Far East? *Why?*

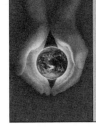

REMEMBER THIS!

When [God] calls you to do something (and He will if you are a believer), He *will* diminish your resources until any hope of success demands a miracle. (p. 34)

WHAT DO YOU THINK?

Gideon armed each man in his token army with nothing more than a ram's horn and a clay jar with a torch in it. Could it be that was a prophetic picture of God's army? We march out to conquer the world armed only with the horn of salvation, our fragile "clay" bodies, and the indwelling light of God's presence leaking out through the cracks of our human brokenness. (p. 33)

Describe instances when God's glory and sufficiency "leaked out" through your personal weakness or insufficiency to touch the life of someone else (almost in spite of you!).

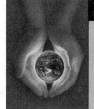

REMEMBER THIS!

I am convinced God never starts until He *doesn't* have enough to begin. (p. 34)

WHAT DO YOU THINK?

If the things to which you feel called do *not* require spiritual resources as well as natural labor, then perhaps you aren't fulfilling your call to its full potential. Don't be surprised if God diminishes your resources until He gets you in the miracle territory. *He values "less" greater than we value "more."* We like fullness; we crave full bellies and full bank accounts. God says, "I value *hunger*. I seek human emptiness in desperate need of My fullness." (p. 34)

1. If "1" represents your natural resources and "10" represents total miracle territory, where are you right now on this "1-to-10 scale" of life resources?

   1   2   3   4   5   6   7   8   9   10

2. Do you feel your resources are diminishing? Is it due to poor stewardship or is God simply trying to call you into His yard to join "His game"?

TAKE IT PERSONALLY!

Man's-eye view says, "That's impossible." God's perspective says, "That's perfect!" Worship is the process of bringing the impossible to Jesus. (p. 35)

MORE ERRONEOUS ASSUMPTIONS, PRESUMPTIONS, AND MISALIGNED PARADIGMS

Jesus reduced the disciples' options until they had nothing to work with but sheer faith.

The amazing part of the process is that *God will even agree with your vision while He's diminishing your resources.* He will say, "Yes, that is the vision—reach for the impossible. Dare to do the unimaginable!" *even as He carefully removes or neutralizes* all of the natural strengths, resources, gifts, and abilities you've come to count on. The quicker you worshipfully say, "I can't," the sooner He majestically says, "But I can." (p. 36)

It seems that many Christians have very odd or narrow understandings about God's nature and the way He interacts with them.

1. We know that Jesus said God is good,[4] but did He ever say anything about God being so "simple" that He must work on only one level or aspect of a problem at a time? How does God interact with you at different levels?

2. If you really believe that God is capable of agreeing with your vision while diminishing your natural resources at the same time, how will it affect your life today and tomorrow?

REMEMBER THIS!

The day you say, "I can't do that," He will move to fill your emptiness with His fullness. The abundance of Deity will flood the lack of your humanity, and a miracle will come to pass before your eyes. This is the process God uses to manifest His will on earth *through us* as it is in heaven. (p. 36)

FILLING THE VOID

The answer is that ____ does *not* get glory from _____, calamity, or _____. He gets glory from our _____, _____, and _____ from the dead through _____ _____. Our heavenly Father truly sees the _____ from the ____. (p. 38)

MORE ERRONEOUS ASSUMPTIONS, PRESUMPTIONS, AND MISALIGNED PARADIGMS

"God, You're late."

"No, I am never late."

"But, God, the church has gone down to nothing. We're going to fall. Aren't You going to catch us?"

"Falling is as important to your maturity and destiny as walking. Remember, I am never late. 'Unless a grain of wheat falls into the ground and dies, it remains alone; but if it dies, it produces much grain.'"[5] (p. 39)

1. Can you remember times when you silently or consciously accused God of "being late" in your life or circumstances? (Describe some of them, and explain how things turned out.)

2. Is there any instance or event in your Christian life when you "fell" due to God's lack of provision? Have you ever "fallen on your face" or "backward on your derriere" due to the failure of your own strength or through your own choices? Explain.

3. Did your "falls" produce humility and furthered destiny or pride and spiritual stagnation in your life?

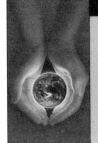

REMEMBER THIS!

The rugged territory between *having enough* and *not having enough* features the same geography as the place between the *already promised* and the *not yet received*. If it were up to us, we would choose the easier path and live on one side or the other. It isn't up to us. (p. 40)

WHAT DO YOU THINK?

God put us in the middle on purpose. He carefully plants us in places of destiny where our pain, our faith, and our passion collide with His abundance, faithfulness, and compassion. Everything you've longed for is already promised and paid for in full, but perhaps it hasn't been delivered yet. Heaven's blood-certified check is in the mail.

By God's design, you and I are positioned and pressed to constantly put a demand on His infinite resources. (p. 40)

1. Do you believe that God really put you in "the middle" on purpose? Explain.

2. If God has placed you there, describe the times your "pain, faith, or passion" collided with His abundance, faithfulness, or compassion.

3. Do you feel positioned to place a demand on God's infinite resources? Why?

NOTES

NOTES

3

NO
P.D.A.

PASSION POLICE ON PATROL

It is time for God Chasers everywhere to make a decision. When it comes to public displays of adoration for our God, we have important news for self-appointed passion police and every religious hall monitor lurking around the corners of a worship gathering: we have a license, signed in blood. It certifies God's covenant and our commitment to fan the flames of our first love from now through eternity. (pp. 45–46)

Virtually every adult who ventures back into the memoried halls of the hometown high school knows the feeling that stalks them from the moment they walk through the front door. Time reverses for a brief moment and you once again feel as you did "back then," when you were just a student under the piercing gaze of the principal or the vice principal.

Some of us still get that feeling every time we toy with the idea of raising our hands toward heaven or fight to hold back hot tears of passion for God in a formal church service. It's time to shake off the memories and restraints of the past. We are new creatures in Christ, redeemed for His good pleasure and anointed to praise Him—regardless of any man-made religious traditions forbidding uninhibited and public displays of adoration and worship.

ERRONEOUS ASSUMPTIONS, PRESUMPTIONS, AND MISALIGNED PARADIGMS

Thanks in part to years of official indoctrination, public displays of affection tend to embarrass us—even when they are legitimate. We can become so zealous and uncomfortable about P.D.A. that we squelch passion because of public scrutiny. (p. 45)

1. Name some of the situations, events, or locations in which public displays of affection (or adoration of God) are considered inappropriate. In your opinion, are these taboos "set in concrete," regardless of circumstances or situations?

2. Have you ever felt embarrassed by public displays of affection (P.D.A.), but later realized some of them were totally proper (and that it was *your* response that was improper)? Explain.

3. Would you ask permission before embracing or kissing your spouse or a loved one in an airport terminal after their return from a long trip or dangerous circumstances? Why or why not?

4. Consider the public display of adoration (P.D.A.) shown by the "sinful woman" toward Jesus in Luke 7:36–39. Would you have felt embarrassed by such an extravagant outpouring of passion for Jesus? Are you *still* embarrassed by such outpourings today? If so, why?

WHAT DO YOU THINK?

Yes, I understand the need to help guide, monitor, and limit affectionate displays among young people. However, it is a serious biblical error to allow the same official disapproval and scrutiny of P.D.A. to cross barriers into the spiritual realm.

Sometimes people just decide that they have been called to join God's passion posse, the chosen frozen appointed and anointed to control and curtail any P.D.A.—public display of *adoration*—for Jesus that might make the cooler crowd feel uncomfortable.

These self-appointed and man-anointed religious refrigerants boldly seek every opportunity to stand before a public assembly of worshipers and say, "Cool down. We will tolerate absolutely no P.D.A. in this holy place." (p. 45)

1. Which choice seems to come more naturally to human nature:

   ❏ to say "yes" to God from the position of humble servanthood and childlike worship, or

   ❏ to say "no" to men from the self-appointed position of a superior or moral judge?

Is it easier to be a critic or an artist and performer? (Please explain your answer.)

2. Would you consider it "natural" for someone to require you to give up either your intellectual capacities or your emotional makeup? Aren't they each part of the greater whole that is known as "you"?

Why would God desire purely intellectual assent or agreement as superior to passionate love and adoration?

3. Jesus said, "You shall love the LORD your God with all your heart, with all your soul, and with all your mind."[1] What do you think about His solution to the alleged conflict between intellectual vs. spiritual worship, and worship vs. the Word?

TAKE IT
PERSONALLY!

I want to publicly display my passion toward Him; I have divine permission and the Creator's commission. (And quite frankly I don't need the prior permission or approval of any created man, woman, or spirit.) (p. 46)

MORE ERRONEOUS ASSUMPTIONS, PRESUMPTIONS, AND MISALIGNED PARADIGMS

When the prophet Elisha put his hands on the king's hands, he was illustrating the process of spiritual instruction, guidance, and coaching. He said, "I don't want you just to shoot the arrow—anyone can do that. Put your hands on the bow . . . now *let me put my hands over yours.*" . . .

The king must have thought, *Who is this frail old man to tell me how to shoot an arrow?* But the prophet was about to mentor him in a whole new level of warfare. Elisha would introduce him to the realm of real power, where the uncallused hands of an aging prophet were more dangerous than a warrior king's practiced hands of war. (p. 47)

One of the most dangerous paradigms and trends for the "me" generation in the church is rooted in the idea that the wisdom and counsel of older and more mature saints is "irrelevant, outdated, and unnecessary."

1. When an older Christian attempts to help you in some area of your life, in what ways are your thoughts similar to those expressed by King Joash in this fictitious mental dialogue from *God's Eye View*?

2. Describe one or more instances in which you realized you had misjudged a Christian leader, parent, or coworker based on their outward appearance or apparent lack of qualification in some area.

3. Do you know an older Christian whose real-life credentials in prayer, the Word, or spiritual insight make them "more dangerous than a warrior king's practiced hands of war" in terms of spiritual warfare or power? If so, describe this person.

WHAT DO YOU THINK?

King Joash couldn't even *see his target*—he should have taken that as a warning sign because the battle wasn't in the physical realm. It would take the practiced hands of a prayer warrior to aim the arrow. This was an elevated battlefield, not of earth but of heaven.

How is it that an action in the seen realm has such eternal significance in the unseen? (pp. 47–48)

1. Describe instances in which you know there is such a thing as "an elevated battlefield, not of earth but of heaven."

2. Describe the spiritual battles you have experienced at that level.

3. Describe events in your own life that seem to confirm that "an action in the seen realm" may have eternal significance in the unseen realm.

MORE ERRONEOUS ASSUMPTIONS, PRESUMPTIONS, AND MISALIGNED PARADIGMS

The last thing Joash expected from his meeting with the dying prophet was a command that made him look foolish right in front of everyone . . . He found it impossible to believe the total defeat of his enemies depended upon a ludicrous action more suited to a madman than a valiant man. (p. 49)

Have you ever become "too religious for your own good"? It happens when we least expect it, and nearly always when we are least prepared for the consequences.

1. What expectations do you have when you meet a "famous" or "nationally recognized" Christian leader or minister? Do you somehow expect them to have a level of perfection greater than "normal" people?

2. When has an event in your life that originally seemed senseless or unpleasant turned into "a blessing in disguise," or "an act of God"?

3. How is it possible for God to work in your life through negative circumstances, embarrassing situations, or painful failures (even if He did *not* cause or instigate them)?

4. Describe some biblical precedents or examples that support your views.

PERSONALLY!

(If these words directed toward the biblical character of King Joash in *God's Eye View* also apply to you, then take them personally!)

But you held your passion in check!

You were polite instead of passionate, and you missed the moment of your greatest victory!

You were more concerned with your dignity than with the will of Deity. (pp. 51–52)

MORE ERRONEOUS ASSUMPTIONS, PRESUMPTIONS, AND MISALIGNED PARADIGMS

We are too quick to assume that God would never deal with us in the same way He dealt with King Joash. That is a dangerous assumption based more on lowered human expectation than on the eternal principles of God's Word.

When the worship leader or pastor steps up to a microphone and says, "It's time to pray," or "It's time to worship," we should *know* that in that moment the eternal law of sowing and reaping is activated. *The passion with which we respond in the spiritual realm almost certainly predetermines our victory in the physical realm.*

All too often, we allow our destiny to be sabotaged by the passion police roaming the halls of worship. (pp. 52–53)

1. Perhaps some of the problem is rooted in our misunderstanding of the "law of sowing and reaping," which obviously (choose one):

    ❑ Applies primarily to the agricultural realm, including the activities associated with farming, ranching, and fruit cultivation.

    ❑ Is limited mostly to financial issues, especially in the areas of tithes and offerings and faith for financial blessings.

    ❑ Has nothing to do with prayer, which is purely spiritual.

❏ Applies to virtually every realm of existence—the natural realms of human relationships, the workplace, and finances; and to the areas of prayer, intimacy in worship, and the study and application of the Word of God in faith.

2. We should realize that God just might deal with us in the same way He dealt with King Joash (using natural actions by command of the Spirit to impact the supernatural and the natural realms). This is because when God said, "I am the Lord, I do not change," He *really* meant to say:

❏ "I am the Lord, and I usually don't change, except in certain circumstances and with certain people."

❏ "I am the Lord, and I constantly change to match the changing cultures emerging in humanity."

❏ "I am the Lord; I do not change."

WHAT DO YOU THINK?

If the people ever realized that they hold the arrows of prophetic destiny in their passionate praise and fervent worship, I suspect the sleepiness would vanish and apathy would give way to a thunderous display of passion. (p. 53)

What would happen if this happened in your home? In your church? In your city? Within the walls of your state capitol?

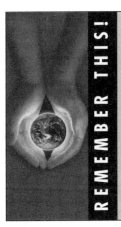

REMEMBER THIS!

We must discard the foolish assumption that God has changed. He still regards passion and brokenhearted entreaty while shelving the unappetizing formalities of lukewarm religious pageantry. Victory is only one arrow of passion away . . .

When you put your hand to the plow of worship, there is *more* involved than just your hand. God lays His hand over yours. When you lay your hands on the sick, you need what is in *His* hand, not what is in yours. It's mentoring by the Master! (p. 53)

WHAT DO YOU THINK?

We miss the whole process of worship and divine habitation when we come in and find contentment sitting among the passionless on church pews or padded seats. We go through the usual religious motions of singing our favorite songs and performing the standard spiritual calisthenics that produce no lasting fruit. (p. 55)

1. Are you satisfied to spend the rest of your life filing into church services week after week, finding contentment among the passionless? Why or why not?

2. Where did God reward passionless people in the Bible?

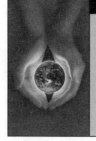

REMEMBER THIS!

For too long we've pulled back in fear every time we heard the "school-marm spirit" whispering to our assembly of worship, "No P.D.A.! No P.D.A.!" The sad truth is that the whole time we've had the license for passionate worship in our pockets. Jesus paid for it with His own blood. (p. 58)

MORE ERRONEOUS ASSUMPTIONS, PRESUMPTIONS, AND MISALIGNED PARADIGMS

Passion stands reluctantly at the door saying, "I can't believe they had Him in this house and no one told me about it. I don't think I'm really welcome here." The problem is our official discouragement of P.D.A. in our religious meetings.

Sometimes we try to hold God captive in a room full of status-preserving disciples while hungry-hearted worshipers search for Him in vain.

. . . We should be like this woman in Simon's house. She knew the whole purpose of that meal was to feed the hunger of God, not satisfy the cravings of man. (pp. 59–60)

Circle true or false for each statement, then explain your choice below:

1. T / F   It might be said that presumption (in the form of anti-P.D.A. policies and procedures) can transform a house of praise and prayer into a house of rigid restriction dominated by religious Pharisees.

2. T / F   "Feeding" is supposed to take place in our meetings, but God simply asks that we set the first place for Him rather than plan the meal around man while minimizing His favorite feast or leaving it off the menu altogether.

TAKE IT
PERSONALLY!

I feel passion welling up in me as I write these words. I'm doing my best to maintain my dignity, but you don't know what He's done for me this week! No one has any right to tell me how passionate I can or cannot be about my Redeemer and healer.

I don't want to know any more *about* Him than I can know *of* Him. Ever since my encounter with His presence, my heart's cry has changed. (pp. 60–61)

WHAT DO YOU THINK?

We don't understand what happens when He comes to church. Seemingly all we do is talk *about* Him when He longs for us to talk *to* Him . . .

Do you feel uncomfortable if a few tears trickle down your face? Do you struggle to maintain your composure when passion finally captures your heart in His presence? It was probably because somebody said, "No P.D.A." Why should you try to hold back the tears? Why would you want to maintain your composure if He's in the house? He came for your worship and hunger, not for your wisdom and religious protocol. God isn't interested in our perfection; He is after our passion. (p. 61)

1. Do the questions I ask in this paragraph from *God's Eye View* make you feel uncomfortable or do they spark even greater hunger and hope in your heart? Why?

2. What is the Holy Spirit speaking to your heart right now?

MORE ERRONEOUS ASSUMPTIONS, PRESUMPTIONS, AND MISALIGNED PARADIGMS

The church is at a critical juncture right now; a divine window in time has been opened. We choose our destiny by what we pedestal and prioritize, and God wants us to choose between Him and our religious ideas *about* Him. (p. 62)

1. Some people are offended by any implication that we have the ability to choose our destiny. I ask then, *does the cry of Joshua to the distracted and double-minded Israelites still ring true today in the church*: "Choose for yourselves this day whom you will serve . . ."?? Explain.

2. Very few Christians wrestle with the temptation to worship household gods crafted from wood and stone, but can you describe some of the modern false gods and idolatries seeking a higher place and pedestal than the things God put first in His Word?

TAKE IT
PERSONALLY!

This is our opportunity to overcome our complacency and make Mary's choice. It is time for us to drop every distraction and religious work to position ourselves at His feet. This is our chance to become the generation that said yes. Destiny awaits our decision. (p. 63)

WHAT DO YOU THINK?

The arrows of deliverance are in your hand. What are you going to do? How will you react? Passionately go for it. You will never know what can happen every time you strike a blow—unless you *do it.*

How many spiritual strongholds will be shattered in your moment of Spirit-breathed passion? Have you asked the fire of God to consume you? Then break free from the spirit of intimidation and loose your passion for His presence. Declare with David, "I will be even more undignified than this!" (p. 64)

Will you "go for it" and pursue Him by faith? Will you dare to strike when God says strike and worship when the Holy Spirit says worship? Are you willing to be become "more undignified" and loose your passion for Him? What do you think you will find if you pour yourself out before God?

NOTES

4

DISCOVER THE POWER OF POSITION

SASHAYING INTO GOD'S PRESENCE

If we ever hope to understand how God works in our lives and churches,
then we must realize that although God is no respecter of persons, He is
a respecter of position. It is one thing to make your petition with passion
and persistence. It is another thing to make your petition from the right
position.

The simple truth is, there is more power in the word *Daddy* than in
the word *Mister.* (p. 67)

The history books speak of many children who managed to disregard every restriction or prohibition placed between them and their famous or politically powerful parents. It happened often in the White House in Washington, D.C., and it happens every day on a smaller scale across the land.

The secret of their power rests in their relationship to the powerful and privileged, not in their inherent power or political prowess. The children of presidents and kings hold a higher rank than the most powerful of politicians and cabinet members because they have a legal place of residence in the hearts of their parents. So it is with God and His sons and daughters.

WHAT DO YOU THINK?

She kept up the badgering, but it didn't work. She had the persistence—and I suppose you might say she had the passion—for what she hoped to possess. Yet she was missing one all-important ingredient: she lacked the power of *position* . . .

This concept of belonging births a totally different valuation process in the heart of a father. If I turned around and saw that one of *my* little girls was looking at something on the shelf, I would have a totally different attitude and mind-set if she came to me and asked, "Daddy, could I have this?" (p. 66)

1. Is God moved more by persistence, passion, or position? Why?

2. What happens if you possess and demonstrate all three?

ERRONEOUS ASSUMPTIONS, PRESUMPTIONS, AND MISALIGNED PARADIGMS

I passed my youngest daughter's bedroom a while back, and I could hear her and another little friend whispering in conspiratorial tones. Naturally I stopped to listen in. (Every parent knows that when a parent passes by his child's bedroom, notices the door is cracked open, and overhears conspiratorial whispering, then it's legal to eavesdrop.)

My daughter was telling her little friend, "I want you to stay and eat dinner with us."

My daughter appeared in the doorway on cue just a few minutes after I'd passed her door. Once she made sure I was seated where I could see her performance, she *sashayed* into the room and sidled up next to me. With a strategic lean into my shoulder, she said, "I love you, Daddy." I was careful to pretend that I was incredibly busy, but I was enjoying every moment of it. "I love you too." (pp. 67–69)

Is this outrageous behavior or totally acceptable "privileged pursuit" in the context of relationship? What is the difference between the two?

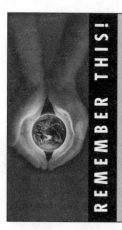

REMEMBER THIS!

In our earthbound daily schedules, we tend to neglect one of the most powerful gifts God has given us as our heavenly Father. His desire for our worship amounts to a permanently open door to the presence of God, and Jesus' sacrifice on the cross gave us an incredible *power of position* that can come no other way. (p. 72)

MORE ERRONEOUS ASSUMPTIONS, PRESUMPTIONS, AND MISALIGNED PARADIGMS

We don't understand that our heavenly Father has no problem supplying our needs. He owns all of the resources of the universe. But He cannot or will not create praise and worship for Himself. He has chosen to rely on *you and me and the rest of the redeemed* for this rarest of commodities. That means His greatest problem is getting us to worship Him from our hearts. (pp. 72–73)

Could it be that we find it hard to believe God has no problem supplying our needs because we think He is like us?

1. Think of the problems He faces "getting us to worship." Note some of them here.

2. Imagine what it would be like for you if, every time you prayed or worshiped Him, He exhibited the same reluctance, self-centered ways, and lukewarm attitudes we display before Him service after service. How would you feel?

TAKE IT
PERSONALLY!

[Your heavenly Father] has been walking through the hall of time, and He eavesdrops in the doorway of your life. He has already heard your request. (p. 73)

WHAT DO YOU THINK?

Sashaying little girls in Louisiana come across as irresistibly cute, but sashaying mortals look simply pitiful by heaven's lofty standards—with one all-important exception. In your heavenly Father's eyes, your pitiful attempts to love on Him *are* virtually irresistible to Him. Oddly enough, the more pitiful and broken you are, the more He is drawn to you.

He knows how often and how hard we battle with secret plots, wrong motives, and bad attitudes. That is where the blood comes in. We are blood kin. The crimson tide of Jesus' cleansing blood *covers* us at our worst as long as we enter God's kitchen as His children with broken and contrite hearts.

. . . I read somewhere that an apostle who thought he was a failure said, "[God] said to me, 'My grace is sufficient for you, for My strength is made perfect in weakness.' Therefore most gladly I will rather boast in my infirmities, that the power of Christ may rest upon me."[1] He rested on the strength of his weaknesses' ability to access God! (pp. 73–74)

1. Explain why it is possible that your weaknesses, faults, and brokenness may actually make you more lovely and lovable in God's eyes.

2. Is it offensive or actually true that you sometimes "battle with secret plots, wrong motives, and bad attitudes" as a flawed human accessing the grace of your perfect Savior? Explain your answer.

FILLING THE VOID

The truth is that your loving _____ _____ has no intention of *not*
_____ your prayer. He is determined to _____ out the encounter and
trade ___ _____ for your _____ and worship—petition for passion.
From an earthly _____, at times it seems our heavenly Father even
_____ that He is incredibly ____ and doesn't hear the request.
Will we ask again? Will we _____ in the _____ _____ for
His favor and _____? (Deity waits for humanity's affirmation: "Yes, I will
____ ___ while it is still early.")[2] (p. 74)

TAKE IT
PERSONALLY!

What happens if we barge into God's kitchen with the demand, "Give me my allowance,
Dad. I want my promised inheritance right now"? Demands have never gone over well with
parents on earth or with our Father in heaven. (p. 75)

WHAT DO YOU THINK?

However well my daughter fared in the shopping department that day, she was
measuring her success according to the only measuring stick available to her
in her immaturity. She equated moments with Daddy with the blessings she
brought back with her.

Who received the real benefit? Was it the daughter who returned with stuffed shopping bags or the father who filled his heart with his daughter's love and his memories with lifelong snapshots of unforgettable shared moments? . . .

A father's blessings provide objective evidence of the power of position . . . As much as I love being around young people, it was the position and power of a *daughter* that influenced me to abandon my pastor friends. (p. 78)

1. Explain how, in a practical way, my daughter's "bagged blessings" provided objective evidence of the power of position.

2. What would influence Deity to spend time with you or with your church family?

MORE ERRONEOUS ASSUMPTIONS, PRESUMPTIONS, AND MISALIGNED PARADIGMS

Much of the time we come to church and begin to worship with the thought rolling around in our minds, *We need this blessing, and we need that one too.* In the process, some of us move beyond seeking His blessings and begin to bless the Blesser.

When we leave services like that healed and whole, or if He touches our emotions and removes the cloud of depression and worry in the midst of our praise, we tend to pick up our stuff from the blessing buffet and go home saying, "Oh, that was a good service! I got what I needed."

Someone needs to ask God what *He* thought of the meeting when we forgot to seek His blessings and became enraptured with His face instead. We might be surprised at the heavenly report. (pp. 78–79)

1. How may we correct our seemingly self-centered approach to worship and worship services?

2. How might you divert more attention toward seeking the Blesser than toward merely seeking His blessings?

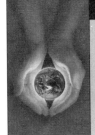

REMEMBER THIS!

There is something special about the divine mix of the power of our position as His children with the power of our passion for His presence that helps satisfy God's desire for worship. (p. 80)

WHAT DO YOU THINK?

Have we constructed a church structure and protocol founded on the blessings instead of the Blesser? In most church services, we spend only enough time in worship to acknowledge our Father's presence before we dive right in to the business of demanding our weekly allowance. (p. 80)

1. Have you ever "timed" your worship services to see where your priorities are? What did you discover?

2. Do you believe it is best to follow a strict protocol in every worship service, or do you believe the Holy Spirit sometimes leads in another direction or a new format? Why do you believe this (include any biblical references you may have)?

MORE ERRONEOUS ASSUMPTIONS, PRESUMPTIONS, AND MISALIGNED PARADIGMS

Every minute of the day, untold millions lift their voices to the invisible God and make petitions in untold languages. As people walk through the store called life, they point out a need or want and begin to ask the Unknown God, "Mister, I need that. I need hope; I need help; I need healing in my marriage, God. I really don't know You, but I need this and that." What they really need is the ability to say, "Daddy." The power of position places their petition on a whole new level.

Once you receive Jesus Christ as Lord and learn the power of your new position with God, everything changes. (p. 80)

1. Why would I say, "What they really need is the ability to say, 'Daddy'"?

2. Why would the "power of position" place someone's petition on a whole new level?

TAKE IT
PERSONALLY!

We must learn the process of leaving one realm to cross into another through the power of position. "You stay in the bedroom; I'm going in the kitchen where Dad is." He is waiting for us to *sashay* into His presence through the process of extravagant and passionate worship. (p. 81)

WHAT DO YOU THINK?

You *enter* His gates with shouts, with singing, and with thanksgiving. That is the first *sashay* as you enter God's kitchen. It is God's way of *getting you off the property of man.*

When you enter His gates, you step onto or into the property of God. Thanksgiving transports you onto the *premises* and under the *promises* of Deity. The first step to move from lowly earth into an exalted and lofty position of intimacy is thanksgiving, "Lord, I'm thankful. We are thankful for what You have done." (p. 82)

1. Is there a "gate" between the property of man and "God's property line"? How do you leave one and enter the other according to the Bible? Explain.

2. Why must you "be on the premises" of God before you come under His promises? (Hint: The privileges of a household are reserved for _____ of the household.[3])

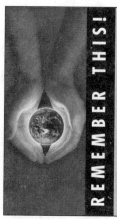

REMEMBER THIS!

If you really want to move into the place of intimacy, you must move beyond the arena where your worship is dictated primarily by what He has done for you. If what you need is more than what He has done in your life, then what you say has to be more than what you've seen Him do. Move beyond the arena of thanksgiving, and *sashay* into the arena of praise . . . (p. 83)

NOTES

NOTES

5

HOW TO MAKE A FOOL OUT OF THE DEVIL

Tattletales Can't Come In

To the earthbound perspective of the human race, this fallen angel still appears larger than life. He promotes the myth that he has the same attributes as God with virtually unlimited knowledge, power, and resources. The truth is, he is literally the tattletale stuck on the porch with a lie in his mouth and a sinking feeling in his heart. (p. 94)

Most of us carry vivid memories of arguments made before the "parental bench," when accusers unfairly (or accurately) pointed the finger of blame in our direction and we countered with desperate arguments or claims of innocence.

One nonhuman accuser in particular has made it his personal mission to condemn us all to hell. God has given us the ability to make a fool out of the devil, but not in the way most of us might assume.

ERRONEOUS ASSUMPTIONS, PRESUMPTIONS, AND MISALIGNED PARADIGMS

The most deadly and persistent of all tattletales can be found practicing his skills on God's front porch in the book of Job. If you carefully examine the way Satan whined to God about Job, then you will realize and remember that he hasn't changed his ways at all. If he whined about Job, you can be sure he and his partners in perdition have built a legal brief on you too. (pp. 85–86)

If you consider the views of the majority of people around you at work, at school, or in your community, they believe the devil (choose one):

❑ Doesn't really exist, except in the form of myth and fanciful religious traditions.

❑ Probably exists, but that he doesn't really have any interest in our affairs (except for the people who really worship him).

❑ Really exists, and that he is the "opposite" of God just as light is the opposite of darkness, hot is the opposite of cold, and good is the opposite of evil.

❑ Exists, and that he works tirelessly to steal, kill, and destroy humanity and anything connected to the kingdom of God (but he is just a fallen angel who was created by God and already sentenced in the Bible).

(The scary part is that you will probably get answers from all four categories in the typical Sunday school class, Christian school, or church congregation survey! The only fully correct answer, according to the Scriptures, is answer number 4.)

WHAT DO YOU THINK?

By the time Tattletale Johnny appeared at the front door and rang the doorbell, I was already in the secret place reserved solely for a mother's son and daughter—the place to which he would never gain access in the Tenney home. (p. 88)

1. Do you feel you have a secret place of privileged access with God when the accuser comes around? (Explain why you feel this way.)

2. Do you dread the wrath or anger of God because of your sins? Why or why not?

(If you do, then you should know that "if you do sin, there is someone to plead for you before the Father. He is Jesus Christ, the one who pleases God completely. He is the sacrifice for our sins. He takes away not only our sins but the sins of all the world."[1])

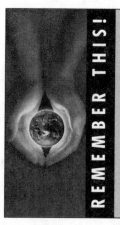

REMEMBER THIS!

There is someone the Bible calls "your adversary" and "the accuser of our brethren, who accused them before our God day and night."[2] This tattletale of tattletales works at his job 24/7, and he has been perfecting his craft over multiple millennia. He is a liar and the father of lies, whose "native language" is untruth.[3] (p. 88)

MORE ERRONEOUS ASSUMPTIONS, PRESUMPTIONS, AND MISALIGNED PARADIGMS

He knows the path to your Father's front porch because it used to be the home address for him and his gang of losers too. He doesn't live there anymore, though . . .

The celestial tattletale is in the same predicament that Johnny Tattletale faced in my neighborhood. He doesn't have any family privileges anymore. It means that he's stuck outside the front screen door, the barrier designed to keep out pests, bugs, snakes, and *used sin* salesmen. (pp. 88–89)

1. How do you view Satan? Is he "bigger than life" in your mind?

2. Do you often feel powerless when confronted with his schemes, hatred, or devious dealings against you or those you love? Explain.

3. If Satan really is just a tattletale with a limited future outside the pit, then how are you living victoriously, worshiping God, and serving others in Christ's name?

4. How should this knowledge impact the daily lives of Christians?

FILLING THE VOID

The _____ is feeling _____ and hungry for _ ____. His sole goal is to ____ _____ to the ear of your heavenly _____ before you gain _____. *He* _____ *you* doing something or harboring unforgiveness. Now he has prepared an airtight brief guaranteed to ____ a _____ _____ and a conviction, and he's ready for the fast dash to the _____ ____ of heaven's porch. He hopes the _____ of God will fall, and you will be _____ ____ to him for _____.[4] (It's the torment that attracts him, not the justice.) (pp. 89–90)

WHAT DO YOU THINK?

For your part, you know you were caught in the act. You have no defense and no intention of preparing one. God has provided something much better for you. Are you ready for the race down the block of life? . . .

What are you going to do? Will you bolt for the nearest church building, pastor's house, or confessional? No, you have privileged access to the very heart of God. Your living Way is not limited to any geographical location or outer perimeter. Three words secure your safety: *"God, forgive me!"* (p. 90)

1. Have you ever thought about this issue before now? (Describe your thoughts if you have—explain *why* if you have not.)

2. When you sin (and I'm positive you do from time to time by virtue of your fallen nature), *what do you do* afterward? (Be honest and "sin not" with your answer.)

3. What *should* you do according to the New Testament Scriptures?

MORE ERRONEOUS ASSUMPTIONS, PRESUMPTIONS, AND MISALIGNED PARADIGMS

Despite all the efforts of hell and its chief tenant, your simple prayers of repentance beat Satan's accusation to the Father's throne every time. Even before the fallen angel could scratch on the front door, your brief prayer of repentance reached God's ear faster than the speed of light via heart-to-heart dispatch . . .

Since you bear the family name, you have exclusive access to heaven through the back door of the blood of the Lamb. Jesus personally ripped the veil that used to divide imperfect people (that includes *all of us*) from our perfect God. Jesus did it so we could have instant access to divine forgiveness and grace. Worship allows you access to places where Satan is forbidden to go. It takes you places the devil can never go. (p. 91)

1. Many Christians seem to think it takes another major sacrifice to gain forgiveness if they sin. Why is this assumption incorrect?

2. If another person comes to you seeking forgiveness, do you sometimes refuse to forgive them, thinking, *They haven't suffered enough*? Does God think this way according to the Scriptures? To put it another way, Do you want God to think this way when *you* come to Him seeking forgiveness?

3. Does it really matter whether or not Satan's accusation is true if you have genuinely repented of your sin and asked forgiveness in Jesus' name? Why?

WHAT DO YOU THINK?

Our Advocate, Jesus Christ, has the legal right to do something considered totally illegal in every human court of law. He doesn't argue against the evidence. He *destroys the entire record*—including the evidence—of our wrong-doing because he has already taken the punishment for our crime . . .

There is no record of your sin—it has been covered under the blood of Jesus Christ who paid the price for it all. The only problem is that Satan can remember your sins—and he can't do a thing about it. That makes him look like the biggest fool in the universe. (p. 93)

1. Is this all too much to believe, or is it something you have received in your heart and mind as real? Explain how or why you came to this position.

2. Have you ever really thought about this? Why would Jesus have the "right" to destroy the evidence gathered against you? (Hint: He took your sentence upon Himself and p__ the p___ in full on the cross.)

REMEMBER THIS!

The key to the family house is worship. Your worship begins the moment you repent of your sins and receive Jesus Christ as Lord and Savior. It continues every time you call upon His name. (p. 93)

MORE ERRONEOUS ASSUMPTIONS, PRESUMPTIONS, AND MISALIGNED PARADIGMS

The devil started high but ended low. He started out as an archangel at the throne, was demoted to prince of the air, ate dust, became Beelzebub (lord of the flies), and winds up in a bottomless pit. I would say that stock in Lucifer, Inc. is tending downward. (p. 94)

Why or how do the actions of people in the church actually "inflate" Satan's stock and the effectiveness of his schemes in their lives and in the world?

❏   They buckle under to peer pressure from unbelievers around them who scoff at any mention of the devil, and ridicule anyone who admits to believing he exists and is at work in the world (he works best among those who don't believe he exists).

❏   As "thoroughly modern" church attenders, they have no problem attending brief church services once in a while, but they've acquired a cynical attitude toward anything overtly "spiritual" or "supernatural" and call it "spooky."

❏   They view the Bible as an outdated and mostly mythical and mystical book of religious teachings, but not necessarily as the inspired Word of God. Therefore, any mention of the devil or Satan is also considered "mostly mythical and mystical" rather than a factual and accurate picture of reality in the spirit realm.

❏   They believe the Bible is the inspired Word of God, but they don't read it or understand it.

❏   All of the above.

WHAT DO YOU THINK?

Do you know the *real* reason that Satan is after you? I hate to burst your balloon, but you are not the ultimate prize he seeks. You are just a pawn. His real purpose is to use your failures and sins to embarrass your Father in heaven. The enemy hurts you only because he hopes to hurt God through the love He has for you. The good news is that the accuser can't win if we run to our Father first. (p. 95)

1. Did the statements in this paragraph catch you by surprise? Why or why not?

2. Given the depths of Satan's hatred for God, how much do you think the enemy hates you and other God Chasers?

3. If your pursuit of your Father's presence draws you closer to Him moment by moment, just how far do you think Satan and his cohorts can afford to follow you?

4. What does that say about the safety available in His presence?

MORE ERRONEOUS ASSUMPTIONS, PRESUMPTIONS, AND MISALIGNED PARADIGMS

Every hour of every day, children of the King step out on God's porch to do the unthinkable. Trapped in the depths of spiritual amnesia, forgetting the countless times they burst through the back door in search of their Father's forgiveness, these blood-washed and forgiven Christians step out on the porch to accuse their siblings and help the father of lies get his story across! . . .

When you stand outside the door of grace to accuse a brother or sister, you are doing Satan's job for him. When you start saying, "God, did You see what so-and-so did?" you are trying to remind God of things that He says don't exist. We don't need any more discouragers; we need some encouragers. (p. 96)

1. Even fervent God Chasers may yield to the temptation to "step out on the porch of accusation" to help Satan lodge a complaint against a believer (especially the self-appointed passion police in the church). Are you guilty of "crossing over" for a griper's feast or "believer's roast" on God's front porch? Explain.

2. Does God really ever need our help locating and pinpointing sin in the church? Why do we insist on "putting in our two cents' worth" anyway?

3. What is our proper role in the church? Where proper discipline takes place in the church, what differentiates it from mere gossip, slander, and vain accusation? (Hint: Personal involvement in the problem, proper authority, a pure motive to restore relationships, and correct biblical steps of communication.)

TAKE IT
PERSONALLY!

God knows which people are on His porch and why they are there. The moment we decide to speak against a brother or sister in Christ, we have stepped on the front porch in the company of the other accuser—and God is listening. I can't imagine a worse place for a child of God. (p. 99)

WHAT DO YOU THINK?

Peter was blessed when he declared the deity of Christ from *inside* the house and recognized the Son of God was on a divine mission from the Father. Everything was fine until Peter stepped to the other side of the screen door to criticize the Son of God as if He were a mere man sending Himself to an early death for merely human reasons . . .

Deity's answer to Peter's critical knock from the porch of accusation was swift and blunt. You are known by those with whom you associate. The moment Peter left Jesus to join Satan as a presumptuous accuser of Divinity, he took on Satan's name as well as his game. Peter ceased to act like a friend of God and took on a new reputation the moment he joined Satan's effort to stop Jesus' progression toward the cross. (p. 100)

1. We look at Peter's big blunder and shake our heads in amazement, but have *you* ever caught yourself criticizing God in some way, whether in conversation to someone else or simply in your private thoughts? Explain.

2. Do you realize that you duplicate Peter's sin every time you criticize or complain about the way God is working in your life through current situations? What are you going to do about it?

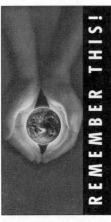

REMEMBER THIS!

Do you want heaven's perspective on your sin and Satan's efforts to shout it from God's front porch? Your heavenly Father knows all about the devil's sour tattletale agenda. He knows every technique in Satan's moth-eaten bag of tricks, and He is always ready to help you make a fool out of the devil. (p. 101)

NOTES

NOTES

THE PRINCIPLE OF MAGNIFICATION

MAKE MOUNTAINS INTO MOLEHILLS OR TURN MEN INTO GRASSHOPPERS

Perhaps your problems seem so big because your altitude is so low. It is time to put the power of magnification into action for good and not for evil. Full understanding may come later; right now you just need to practice it. (p. 113)

The biblical story of the "ten Israelite spies who said no" portrays a virtual breakdown of destiny at the edge of the Jordan River. Since that event, countless Jews and Christians faced with a challenge of faith have turned to this story of doubt and unbelief versus faith and courage for guidance.

It all boils down to the principle of magnification. Whatever you magnify with your heart and mouth determines the direction of your destiny—it will lead you forward into the frontier of faith or backward into the shadows of doubt.

ERRONEOUS ASSUMPTIONS, PRESUMPTIONS, AND MISALIGNED PARADIGMS

Many Christians allow circumstances to determine their level of worship when worship should really be disconnected from circumstances. If you allow the conditions of life to dictate your level of worship, they will also determine and limit your altitude. The only way to achieve the altitude of God's eye view is found in this passage: "Those who *wait* on the LORD . . . shall mount up with wings like eagles."[1] (p. 102)

Circle true or false for each statement:

1. T / F   When we allow circumstances to determine the altitude of our worship, we are like the man described by James the apostle who was "double-minded" and unstable in all his ways. He said, "He who doubts is like a wave of the sea driven and tossed by the wind."[2]

3. T / F   Our worship should be disconnected from circumstances because the One we worship dwells and rules above all circumstances.

3. T / F   Worship possesses the power to change the way we deal with changing circumstances.

4. T / F   All we have to do is "fake it" in bad times. Faking faith is the secret to success.

5. T / F   We don't have to "fake it" with God. Even Moses, King David, the Old Testament prophets, and the disciples confessed or demonstrated their fear in times of crisis—God's faithfulness is not dependent merely upon our faith. As we praise and worship Him, our faith grows stronger because we *magnify* Him and allow Him to become greater in our eyes than our problems.

WHAT DO YOU THINK?

David the psalmist declared under the anointing of God, "Oh, *magnify* the LORD with me."[3] He was referring to worship. If worship *magnifies,* then does its absence minimize?

A young and unmarried but pregnant Jewish woman named Mary echoed David's words centuries later when she declared to her relative who was also expecting a child, "My soul *magnifies* the Lord, and my spirit has rejoiced in God my Savior."[4] What does it mean "to magnify"? (p. 103)

1. What would *you* have done in Mary's place?

2. Do you believe she was "drawing bigger pictures" of an already infinite God, or was she worshiping and praising God with everything within her being?

3. When was the last time you did this? (Why not right now?)

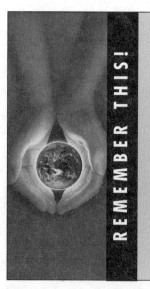

REMEMBER THIS!

When you look through a magnifying glass at a grasshopper, you are not making the grasshopper bigger; you are just making it *appear* bigger. The process of worship does not make God bigger; it just makes Him *appear* bigger.

Unlike the grasshopper, God is already bigger than all created beings, form, and matter; yet the magnification of worship makes Him larger in *your* view. Suddenly everything about Him gets bigger in your eyes. That means His capabilities get bigger, His power gets bigger, and the force of all of His promises and wonder is suddenly enlarged when you magnify the Lord. (p. 104)

MORE ERRONEOUS ASSUMPTIONS, PRESUMPTIONS, AND MISALIGNED PARADIGMS

Why does the world have such a skewed view of God? One of the most important reasons is that we have not magnified God in the sight of the unsaved. They look at our misrepresentations (and underrepresentation) of Him and His kingdom and say, "Nothing we see there can help us. Those people are as messed up as we are."

We must restore the principle of magnification. How do we do that? Worship magnifies God to the world. When they see and hear us praise God for His mighty works and His godly attributes, they begin to realize there is more to Him than meets the eye. When non-Christians hear how He transformed our lives, they begin to see Him for the first time. Then they say, "If He can do that for them, then maybe He would do it for me too." This is the principle of magnification in operation. (pp. 104–5)

All too often, we tend to dismiss the sour attitude of the unsaved toward God by blaming their "sin nature." The truth is that at least part of the blame should come closer to home.

1. If your life is the only "Bible" or gospel message your neighbor will ever see, have you given him or her "the whole story" or has your lifestyle left out most of the pieces? Explain (or discuss the necessary changes).

2. Is it reasonable for nonbelievers to "window-shop" the Christian world to evaluate our "advertising claims" before committing their lives to what we say is truth? Why?

3. Can you blame them for hesitating or openly refusing to buy what we put on display? Explain.

WHAT DO YOU THINK?

God revealed Himself to the son of a moon worshiper and gave him a God-sized promise. Abraham used the rest of his life as a magnifying glass to declare and reaffirm God's power and ability to keep His impossible promise. Countless individuals, tribes, and people groups saw their first glimpse of God through Abraham's worship and faith in God. (p. 105)

1. Does God prefer to work with fourth-generation seminarians from Ivy League universities, or does He appear to freely pick and choose His servant leaders from virtually every area of society? (Hint: See 1 Cor. 1:25–29.)

2. *What about you?* How many people will see their "first glimpse of God" through your worship and demonstrated faith in God? What are you prepared to do about it?

MORE ERRONEOUS ASSUMPTIONS, PRESUMPTIONS, AND MISALIGNED PARADIGMS

Fear also works according to the magnification principle. If faith is the forward gear propelling a car forward, then fear is the reverse gear propelling the same car backward.

Faith and fear operate on the same principle. The alarming thing about it is that North Americans have allowed fear to so infiltrate our version of the English language that we have adopted "fearful language" as a matter of habit. How many times have you asked someone how he is feeling only to hear him say, "I'm afraid I'm catching a cold"?

Job said, "The thing I greatly feared has come upon me, and what I dreaded has happened to me."[5] Have we made that our cultural slogan? (p. 105)

Our unfortunate love affair with "casual Christianity" causes us to underestimate the true importance of our words. Look up and fill in the missing words in these Bible passages about the importance of our words.

1. Brood of vipers! How can you, being evil, _____ ____ _____? For out of the abundance of the heart the _____ _____. A good man out of the good treasure of his heart brings forth good things, and an evil man out of the evil treasure brings forth evil things. (Matt. 12:34–35)[6]

2. But I say to you that for every ____ ____ men may _____, they will give _____ of it in the day of _____. For by ____ _____ you will be _____, and by ____ _____ you will __ _____. (Matt. 12:36–37)[7]

3. A man's stomach shall be satisfied from the _____ __ ___ _____, from the _____ __ ___ ____ he shall be filled. _____ ___ ____ are in the _____ __ ___ _____, and those who love it will eat its fruit. (Prov. 18:20–21)[8]

4. He who would love life and see good days, let him _____ ___
   _____ from ____, and his ____ ____ _____ _____. (1 Peter
   3:10)[9]

5. And ___ _____ __ _ ____, a world of iniquity. The _____ is so set
   among our members that __ _____ __ ____ ____, and ____ _
   ____ the course of nature; and __ _ __ _ ____ by hell. (James
   3:6)[10]

6. But no man can ____ __ _____. It is __ _____ ____, full of
   _____ _____. With it __ _____ our God and Father, and with it
   __ _____ men, who have been made in the similitude of God. Out
   of the ____ _____ proceed blessing and cursing. My brethren, these
   things ought not to be so. (James 3:8–10)[11]

WHAT DO YOU THINK?

*[Continued from the list of revised claims made by the "Backward Boys" (p.
107), the "ten spies who said no" to God's prophetic destiny for Israel . . .]*

3. *All* the people whom we saw in it *are men of great stature* [does
   this include *all* of the tribes previously listed?].
4. There we saw the giants (the descendants of Anak came from the
   giants); and we were like grasshoppers *in our own sight*, and *so we
   were* in *their* sight.[12]

This reminds me of a performance of *Patriarchal Pinocchio* with ten
men sporting extremely long noses. (p. 107)

1. Have you ever run into "Backward Boys" who stepped into a situation with a fear-powered report that discouraged you or others facing a challenge to their faith? If so, explain.

2. Have you noticed how the magnifying power of *fear* seems to expand and enlarge fearful descriptions and encourage even greater attempts to justify our claims and convince others to join in? If so, explain.

TAKE IT PERSONALLY!

Joshua and Caleb focused their eyes on faith and the size of their God instead of the size of their problems. Decide for yourself which one you will look at, but you should realize that God is more than 432 times bigger than your biggest problem. He fills the universe and more. No matter how big your problem appears to be at the moment, your God is bigger still. (pp. 108–9)

WHAT DO YOU THINK?

What does all of this have to do with worship? Worship is the spiritual equivalent of the power of magnification. Magnification possesses the power to *turn mountains into molehills or men into grasshoppers.* Very often we fly over a thunderstorm and land in the sunshine on our ministry trips. We must understand that worship does the same thing. (pp. 110–11)

1. Is this something practical you can use right now, or does this sound like some "pie-in-the-sky" theological concept that won't work in real-life situations? Explain your answer.

2. Are you facing a mountain or insurmountable obstacle in your life right now? Describe it in detail below. Then begin to describe God using every biblical reference and pattern you can find. *Who or what is greater?*

MORE ERRONEOUS ASSUMPTIONS, PRESUMPTIONS, AND MISALIGNED PARADIGMS

Some people think they are too spiritual for songs and worship. They like to say, "Well, I don't know about you, but *I live in the Spirit* all the time. I don't need warm-ups." . . .

I'm happy for people who live on mountaintops all the time, but I'm not one of them. Everyone I've ever known or heard of—including Jesus Christ, Peter, and Paul the apostle—experienced difficult circumstances. (p. 111)

Pride brought down one of God's most gifted and anointed creations. If Lucifer the covering archangel was defiled by proud thoughts about his own abilities and glory, surely we should avoid this soul virus at all costs.

1. How do spiritual songs of praise and worship affect you in difficult times?

2. Why should you worship Him continually instead of waiting until a crisis comes along?

TAKE IT PERSONALLY!

Worship is the wind beneath our wings that lifts us up above the earthly realm. The truth is that if you are "in Him," then there is a place in worship to which you may go and sit with Him on high, and *look down* on the lesser issues below. I call it getting God's eye view of life's circumstances. I know we often speak of getting a bird's-eye view, but wouldn't you prefer to get a God's eye view of the things that concern you? (p. 112)

WHAT DO YOU THINK?

Spread your wings in unhindered worship. Remember that the worship leaders, musicians, and singers are not singing to entertain you. They are revving the engines of praise, worship, and adoration to the Lord so that you can lift off and soar above every weight and encumbrance. You can worship with them, or you can worship without them. Birds don't need each other to fly, but sometimes they do fly together! Whatever your problems may be, worship will help you rise above them and "mount up with wings like eagles." (pp. 113–14)

1. When you catch yourself slipping into the "entertained spectator" mode in worship services or meetings, how do you personally step out of it and return to the "Mary position" of genuine worship and adoration?

2. Explain how you feel worship leaders, singers, musicians could avoid the "entertainer" rut in their roles.

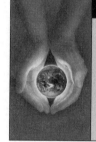

REMEMBER THIS!

Your Creator and Redeemer never intended for you to look at your problems from the lowly perspective of earth—even your smallest problems can *appear* to be overwhelmingly large when you're looking through the wrong end of the perspective telescope. (p. 114)

MORE ERRONEOUS ASSUMPTIONS, PRESUMPTIONS, AND MISALIGNED PARADIGMS

The process of worship takes you higher than anyplace you have ever been. Throw out your padded spectator seats, and put on your game cleats. *Worship is not a spectator sport.* God is about to set you free. This is your moment—rise above the pain; you'll never be the same. *Wait upon Him with your worship,* and rise above the circumstances . . .

"You don't understand. I'm handcuffed; I'm shackled to my circumstance with no hope of escape." Either you can believe your own words and let them become your self-fulfilling prophecy, or you can believe God's Word and wait upon Him until new strength comes from on high. (p. 118)

1. What is the difference between watching worship as a spectator and "waiting" on God as a worshiper?

2. Describe some of the "excuses" that have come to mind or that you have heard to justify remaining in the pain of circumstances or situations (when worship was available and waiting to bring a change of perspective).

TAKE IT
PERSONALLY!

This is just the beginning. Only God knows where your *yes* to His proposal of worship will take you.

He has placed the power of magnification in your hands. It is up to you to use it wisely and effectively. Will you magnify Him and turn your mountains into molehills, or magnify men and live life like a grasshopper? (p. 119)

NOTES

NOTES

RECLAIMING WORSHIP

THE GREATEST MOOD-ALTERING DRUG

Worship is the greatest of all mood-altering drugs. It possesses the power to turn your darkest night into your brightest day. Worship will loose the winds of heaven to lift you on wings of praise into God's presence. Depression, discouragement, grief, and sorrow—they pale in power and influence when you begin to praise God, from whom all blessings flow. (pp. 135–36)

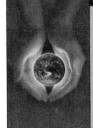

REMEMBER THIS!

Worship is the jugular vein of life in God's kingdom. *If Satan can stop your worship, then he will have access to anything else in your life.* (p. 121)

WHAT DO YOU THINK?

If your brother (or sister) in Christ loses the ability to worship due to the thievery of the enemy, he doesn't need another accuser running up to the Father's front porch saying, "Let me tell You about Your son." He needs someone who will bring a bullock or an oxen and say, "Here, I will help you worship!" He needs someone who will help restore his ability to worship, so complete restoration can come into his life! (p. 122)

1. How well do you feel you have been taught (and practice) the "caring and carrying" aspects of the Christian life (i.e., the New Testament's commands to care for one another and share our burdens)?

2. How is it possible for you to restore someone else's ability to worship God?

ERRONEOUS ASSUMPTIONS, PRESUMPTIONS, AND MISALIGNED PARADIGMS

The LORD shall preserve *your going out* and *your coming in*
From this time forth, and even forevermore.[1]

Here is my affirmation: I've made up my mind that even when I get pulled away from His presence by temporary earthly priorities, I am going to stay close to the door so I can slip back in at any point!

Some people find it easier to enter God's presence than others *because they never sleep far from the door.* They literally stay on the edge of worship. (p. 123)

Mark the statement that best describes your views about "entering God's presence":

❏ I'm not sure *anyone* can enter God's presence. After all, He is God and we are flesh.

❏ I think we can get a little glimpse of it once in a while, but that's about it.

❏ I think it *is* possible to "live and walk in the Spirit" as Paul described in the book of Galatians (5:16, 25).

If you felt the desire to change your "original" answer to another answer as your eye moved down this list of choices, explain why:

FILLING THE VOID

Never look at _____ ___ _ _____ or before a _____'s _____ and say he is the "source of power." The person may be an _____ of _____, but you could say the same thing about a twenty-five-cent _____ outlet or a two-dollar _____ _____ from a discount store . . .

We must remember that anyone we see operating in a _____ _____ or _____ _____ in the church is an _____, not the _____ of the power we see flowing through him. That worship leader may be an outlet for power, and that preacher or teacher may be an outlet, too; however, __ ___ or _____ should be considered *the Source*. (pp. 123–24)

WHAT DO YOU THINK?

Another way to reclaim your stolen magnifying glass is to force your attention and focus away from your circumstances and loss and onto the Lord. This is where my analogy or earthly picture becomes insufficient . . .

You start afresh with what you have. If all you have is one whimper of worship, then give it to Him, and watch Him breathe on it, bless it, and multiply it. (pp. 125–26)

1. Have you ever hesitated to pray or worship because you felt you had too little or nothing to offer God? Describe why you felt that way.

2. Have you ever experienced the thrill of seeing God multiply your "whimper of worship" and bring a new perspective to you? Describe it.

TAKE IT
PERSONALLY!

Discouragement is another diabolical key that opens the door for the thief to steal our goods . . .

I feel the anointing of God to tell you right now, *you will not fail, and I have witnesses to prove it: Samson and Moses.* Pick up where you left off! Restart your worship—reclaim your destiny! (p. 127)

MORE ERRONEOUS ASSUMPTIONS, PRESUMPTIONS, AND MISALIGNED PARADIGMS

As soon as the last enemy fell, Samson made a speech about his accomplishment and promptly tossed away the jawbone. Then, only seconds after the miracle that had just occurred, Samson started complaining to God and magnifying the negative: "You have given this great deliverance by the hand of Your servant; and *now shall I die of thirst and fall into the hand of the uncircumcised?*"[2]

God said, "Don't say you're finished with something before I am finished with it. Now go back to the same place where you just witnessed a miracle if you want another one."[3] Don't be surprised if God tells you to go right back to the last place you had a divine encounter. He told Samson, "I'm not through with you or with the place of the jawbone. Get back there and lift your perspective. Return to the place where you destroyed the enemy, and this time it will be a source of refreshing." The moral of the story is this: *don't say you are finished before God does.* (p. 128)

The first inclination many of us feel after reading something like this passage is to think, *Well, that was Samson, not me. If that kind of miracle happened in my life, I would never act like that.*

1. Have you ever left a really memorable worship service only to find yourself complaining aloud (or under your breath) about something like the broken air conditioner in your car or about your financial situation? If so, what were you complaining about?

2. How are these situations similar to Samson's situation?

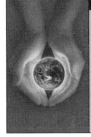

REMEMBER THIS!

When someone steals your magnifying glass, one of the best things you can do is to remember and relive the old victories and deliverances of God in your life. They will remind you that if God has done it once, He can do it again. Don't say you're finished before He says He is finished. (p. 128)

WHAT DO YOU THINK?

God is tired of arm wrestling us for His church, so He'll let us get to the point of desperation where we will just resign and say, "It's Yours, Lord. It is all Yours." That is when He will say, "Good! Now take care of it."

Divine perspective changes everything and helps everything come into divine alignment. At times, the only way God can give you *His* view of your situation is to make you throw down everything that supports and encourages *your* view of life and ministry. (pp. 129–30)

1. One of the clichés that we often hear in the church says, "Let go and let God." Do you feel this is just a cliché, or is there a solid foundation of truth to it? Why?

2. Why would God need to "arm wrestle" us for His church? (Explain in your own words.)

MORE ERRONEOUS ASSUMPTIONS, PRESUMPTIONS, AND MISALIGNED PARADIGMS

How many times has He asked you to throw down your rod of comfort and security? What will you do if He asks you to lay down the security of a nine-to-five job with two checks per month and a liberal bonus package to pursue His impossible dream?

. . . God may not send you against an earthly prince or the head of a modern government, but He will almost certainly send you on a mission far beyond your ability. (p. 131)

1. Describe your "gut reaction" the first time you read the words in the passages quoted above.

2. How do you feel right now about the almost certain prospect of being dispatched on spiritual missions "far beyond your ability"?

3. Does this represent a big change from the way you *used to view* the Christian life? Why?

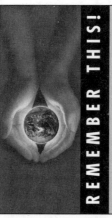

REMEMBER THIS!

I can't tell you how many times I've said, "Please let me quit, God!" By the same token, I can't tell you how many times I *have quit* only to find that *He wouldn't accept my resignation.* He wasn't after a change of office, a change of vocation, or a simple change of address—He wanted to see a genuine *change of heart.* (p. 132)

FILLING THE VOID

When you feel _____ and under_____, you tend to _____ the ____ representing any lingering _____ _____ harder than usual. Throw it down, and _____ your _____, _____, and _____ about His _____ at His feet as well.[4]

If you sense the need to _____ Him but mourn the loss of your magnifying glass, then _____ to the site of your last _____ or divine _____. Throw down the rod of your _____ and _____ in total _____ on _____ (and He will give you something far better). (p. 132)

WHAT DO YOU THINK?

Moses had a change of attitude, and his rod had a change of ownership. Until that moment, Moses had leaned on the stick and called it *his* rod. Everything changed once he obeyed God and threw it down, watched it turn into a snake, and dared to pick it back up at God's command.

Before that moment, the rod was only strong enough for one man to lean on. Afterward, the rod of God represented a covenant relationship so strong that a whole nation depended on it. By God's will, it commanded enough power to open the Red Sea and bring Pharaoh to his knees. It pays to listen and obey when God asks you to release something or to pick up the unexpected. (p. 133)

1. If Moses' obedience with the rod allowed an entire nation to lean on the leadership represented in his divine calling, describe what might happen if you lay down before Him every gift and calling in your life in submission.

2. How might more people be able to lean upon God's investment in your life once you lay down your life at His feet?

MORE ERRONEOUS ASSUMPTIONS, PRESUMPTIONS, AND MISALIGNED PARADIGMS

The unexpected should be expected when God is dealing with the idolatry of the "normal." Illogical requests are perfectly logical when Deity must deal with the human worship of logic and the perfectly predictable. (p. 133)

List some examples of "illogical requests" made in the Old and New Testaments of the Bible.

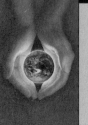

REMEMBER THIS!

In the natural realm, seedtime and harvest have a lot in common. In fact, their only outward difference is *quantity*. If it's not *enough*—*it's seed!* (p. 134)

WHAT DO YOU THINK?

When it is time to plant corn or wheat, you basically have a relatively small pile of seed corn that you put in the ground. At harvest time, the small pile of seed you planted should produce a very large pile of corn or wheat seed . . .

The similarity is that you have the same kind of seed in both piles, only the quantity is different. Look at it this way: when you *don't have enough* seed to live on, as hard as it seems, that is the time to *put it in the ground*. The end result is a great harvest. (pp. 134–35)

1. Describe the areas where you sense you don't have enough resources to sustain you (e.g., finances, physical health, stability in relationships, favor with others, personal knowledge or training).

2. What are you prepared to do with what you have? Will you "plant" it as seed into the field of God's faithfulness? Why?

TAKE IT
PERSONALLY!

Sow a seed of worship when you feel that your world has been reduced to a pile of ashes. God will quickly respond to the emptiness offered through your broken and contrite heart and will magnify Himself in your life and the lives of your friends. (p. 135)

WHAT DO YOU THINK?

When you get the opportunity to sit down with all of the witnesses peering over the balusters of heaven, ask Moses about sowing his rod. Ask David about sowing his prophesied destiny into the difficult soil of decades of patience, trusting by faith that he would reap a harvest of divine purpose in due season. Ask John about sowing his head, and ask Jesus about sowing His life. Ask each of them if it was worth it. Ask them if God was faithful. Now have you relocated your magnifying glass? Worship Him. (p. 135)

1. Does this passage "set you back" in any way? Why?

2. How does the "sowing and reaping" principle in this passage seem to differ from the way you have heard it taught or described in the past?

3. Why is this difference valid and important enough for Christians to consider?

NOTES

NOTES

8

THE POWER OF PROXIMITY

MOVE CLOSER, WHISPER SOFTER

Praise is roughly similar to magnification. Worship, with its characteristic of intimacy and unconditional love, speaks of the power of proximity. When you link magnification of God with proximity or closeness to Him, He fills up your whole screen so that all you see is Him. (p. 138)

WHAT DO YOU THINK?

There are at least two ways to make something bigger to the eye. You can magnify it with a magnifying glass, microscope, or telescope; or you can move *closer* to it. Magnification makes an object *appear* larger to the eye, but there is only one way to get a sense of an object's true size in relation to you. You must move yourself closer or draw it close to you in some way. (p. 137)

1. Why is it biblical (or nonbiblical) to talk about "magnifying" God or "drawing near" to Him when He already fills the universe?

2. Describe instances in your own life when you knew you were magnifying God, and when you sensed His presence had "come near."

REMEMBER THIS!

Everything looks less intimidating when you are perched in Daddy's arms, viewing the world from His eye view. It also puts you in close proximity to Daddy's ear! And there's particular advantage to that position. (p. 139)

ERRONEOUS ASSUMPTIONS, PRESUMPTIONS, AND MISALIGNED PARADIGMS

Have you ever noticed that some people seem to get their prayers answered more than others? It could almost make you suspect that God is a respecter of persons, but He said He isn't.[1] . . .

No, it is not that these people are "better" than you. *They may be closer.* If you can ever get *close,* anything is possible. I sense the Holy Spirit hovering over these words as I write. He's close to you now if you're worshiping as you read! (p. 139)

Have you ever wondered—after seeing others receive answers to prayers or receive blessings when you didn't—if God plays "favorites"?

1. Describe what happened (then and later).

2. How is "being closer" to God different from being "more favored" by God?

3. Do you believe it is possible for *any Christian* to draw closer to God, or is it only reserved for a privileged few? Why?

WHAT DO YOU THINK?

Does God require us to "win and woo" His attention? No, but He *delights* in it. Is it right to butter up God? No, not if you offer Him flattery in place of loving and extravagant worship. The answer is yes if you delight in loving Him and worshiping Him, even while hoping to make a request of Him.

The difference between flattery and worship is that those who flatter God in hopes of wringing a blessing out of Him lack *genuine relationship and privileged position.* (p. 140)

The Bible makes it clear that God hears every word spoken by every person alive at any given moment and that He will hold each of us accountable for what we say. That supports the statement that we don't have to woo Him to get His attention—He's already listening.

In your opinion, does God invite, welcome, and "sit on the throne" created with our praise and worship? Explain your answer. (Hint: Read Ps. 22:3.)

TAKE IT
PERSONALLY!

Many who call themselves Christians have grown accustomed to living their lives feeling as if God was far away from them—an absentee father of sorts.

God often anoints or equips people to lend us their binoculars to help magnify Him in our eyes. When people begin to preach or simply talk about Him and the things He has done in their lives, they allow you a peek through their binoculars. Their magnification glass or spiritual telescope pulls their view and their vision of God up very close to *you*. This is what happened with the Samaritan woman at the well who had a God encounter at Jacob's well. (p. 141)

MORE ERRONEOUS ASSUMPTIONS, PRESUMPTIONS, AND MISALIGNED PARADIGMS

I can't speak for others, but I firmly believe the advice my parents gave me when I was a child: "Always *look* where you are going." Are you looking at Him, or are you looking at your problems, the might of your enemy, or the size of your obstacle? Are you looking at the waves or the Wave Maker? When things get tough, do you move closer to Him or run away from Him? (p. 142)

1. When little children get hurt on a playground or in the backyard, where do they *tend* to keep their eyes even as they cry, run for help, or hold up the place of the injury?

❑ On their wounds

❑ On their friends

❑ On the playmate culprit who committed the crime

❑ On their parents, the ones with the enfolding arms and comforting voices that make everything seem all right

2. When you *get hurt, run into adverse circumstances, or feel threatened,* where do you tend to keep your eyes? Why?

WHAT DO YOU THINK?

Abraham set the vision of faith at the beginning, long before he ever stepped foot on the mountain of God. *If we can ever worship at the height, we can return.* Far too often we get tired of exerting the energy and sacrifice it takes to get to that height.

We decide to settle for secondary ascents and the ease of fast-food service. We opt for the lesser path and hang around the lowlands of low risk and blood-free worship. Then we wonder why we never see the solution to our problems. (p. 146)

1. How would you define "low-risk and blood-free worship"?

2. Is it correct to use words and phrases such as "exert energy" and "sacrifices" when talking about worship? Why or why not?

FILLING THE VOID

_____, and _____ _____ to Him. Tap the power of _____, and you may draw near enough to ___ _____ to receive a ___'_____ view of your mountain. Then you will have the ability to see *both* sides of the mountain and the _____ _____ at the summit. He _____ _____, and He _____ low. "It is He who sits above the circle of the earth, and its inhabitants are like _____."[2] (p. 148)

MORE ERRONEOUS ASSUMPTIONS, PRESUMPTIONS, AND MISALIGNED PARADIGMS

Do you believe God has already spoken to the solution for your problems? It seems the solution often obeys His command better than the problem.

He has spoken to your "ram" as well, and He has predetermined the intersection point where you will meet His provision and solution. It is all laid out, so your job is to listen, obey, and do what it takes to get to that point. Worship Him, and draw near. If He can get you to keep going, you will find His ram waiting for your arrival. (p. 148)

The lives of most Christians are virtually indistinguishable from people who do not serve Jesus Christ because (choose one):

❑   They are doing their best to blend in with the unsaved to become better witnesses for the gospel.

❑   The God they serve isn't strong enough or simply doesn't care enough to help them live richer, more fulfilling lives marked by supernatural love, joy, and peace—even in the midst of changing circumstances.

❑   Most do not believe God has already spoken a solution or that He even cares about their problems.

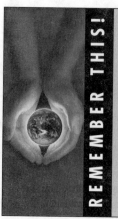

REMEMBER THIS!

You shouldn't be surprised—don't you see it? *He prearranged the rendezvous.* God has been waiting for you to reach the end of your-self so He can reveal *Himself.* Worship takes you from human weak-ness to divine strength, and finally into His glory on the mountain of God's eye view. (p. 149)

WHAT DO YOU THINK?

It seems to me the tree on the mountain of God was just as carefully planted and tended by Deity as was the tree of destiny planted for Zacchaeus in Jericho. Perhaps angelic hands were commissioned to shape the branches of that low-lying tree three millennia or so ago according to the growth template matching the emerging horns of a splendid wild ram who favored the wind-swept place at the top of a mountain in Moriah. Destiny awaited a divine encounter there as well. This carefully crafted tree on Moriah, the land of God's eye view, predated the tree in Jericho and predicted the holy tree on Calvary. (p. 150)

1. Does destiny await a divine encounter with every true believer, or is that a special event reserved solely for special people?

2. Did most of the people described in the Bible experience these "divine encounters with destiny" while they sat in meditation somewhere, or while they were actively pursuing God in some way? What about you? Are you sitting or pursuing?

TAKE IT
PERSONALLY!

Worship is all you need to get to the prearranged intersection, the divine rendezvous of revelation where God waits to speak destiny into your soul and unveil His provision for your pain. (p. 151)

MORE ERRONEOUS ASSUMPTIONS, PRESUMPTIONS, AND MISALIGNED PARADIGMS

The psalmist also wondered who would make the grade as God Catchers:

> *Who may ascend into the hill of the LORD?*
> *Or who may stand in His holy place?*
> *He who has clean hands and a pure heart,*
> *Who has not lifted up his soul to an idol,*
> *Nor sworn deceitfully.*[3]

I am convinced that repentance is the New Testament equivalent of old covenant blood sacrifice. We enter the door of God's kingdom when we confess our sins and receive Jesus Christ the Son of God as our Lord and Savior. While many Christians believe and act as if the process of maturity and discipleship ends there, Jesus taught that it only *begins* there. (pp. 151–52)

The doctrine of salvation by grace is valid and true, but many people in the church believe that grace somehow covers every sin of laziness and apathy in their Christian lives. Others seem to have the mentality that once they receive Jesus Christ as Lord and Savior, that their job is simply to "lay back and let it happen."

Compare these views with the reality in the following Scripture passages:

> *If anyone desires to come after Me, let him deny himself, and*
> *take up his cross daily, and follow Me.*[4]

> *Yes, and all who desire to live godly in Christ Jesus*
> *will suffer persecution.*[5]

> *Show me your faith without your works,*
> *and I will show you my faith by my works.*[6]

How do the human assumptions and paradigms I've described compare to the truths, principles, and insights in these passages from God's Word?

TAKE IT
PERSONALLY!

Things shouted at our Father from a distance don't affect Him like praises or wishes whispered in His ear up close. I am convinced that the next genuine revival will be a revival of intimacy. (p. 152)

MORE ERRONEOUS ASSUMPTIONS, PRESUMPTIONS, AND MISALIGNED PARADIGMS

At its best, the power of proximity transforms us into *microphones* in God's hands, magnifying and amplifying His authoritative voice and life-giving touch in the earth. The closer you get to Him, the louder you sound to the devil and the more powerful is your witness among people. But if it is not Him, all you amplify is your own ineptness. (p. 154)

Your life *will* magnify something, whether or not you approve it or seek it. What message is your life sending to the world?

❑ God and I are really close . . . on weekends, during religious holidays, and in times of crisis.

❑ I'm a Christian, but I'm not very happy about it. It doesn't make much difference in my life as you can see.

❑ I'm a closet Christian and I'm determined to fit into the world so I won't feel rejection or suffer the consequences for being so "religious."

❑ Jesus Christ saved and transformed my life and I will never be the same. Don't wait around for me to "get better" or "get over it." I'm just going to "get worse" and "go deeper," and my life is an unending adventure with the One who loves me more than any other. *Talk to me if this is the life you long for.*

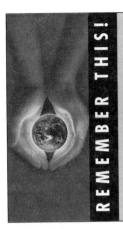

REMEMBER THIS!

It is time to worship, but not the wimpy worship that stops simply when the clock hits twelve noon. It is time to worship your way to Moriah, the land of God's eye view. Worship and praise your way up the mountain of the Lord, and don't settle for anything less than a mountaintop encounter with the joy of your heart's desire. (p. 155)

WHAT DO YOU THINK?

If your Christian life lacks power, you won't find it in a formula or "seven *easy* steps to Christian success." You will find it in determined praise, uninhibited repentance and surrender, and the willingness to worship your way all the way onto God's altar and into close *proximity* to His heart.

I think I know what you're thinking, but I read somewhere, "I beseech you therefore, brethren, by the mercies of God, *that you present your bodies a living sacrifice, holy, acceptable to God,* which is your reasonable service."[7] (p. 155)

1. What *were* you thinking when you read this passage?

2.If you were hoping that all the necessary sacrifices were taken care of on Calvary, what do you think now that it's clear God expects you to present *yourself* as a living sacrifice to Him? Are you ready?

NOTES

NOTES

9

CLAIM YOUR BACKSTAGE PASS

WORSHIP YOUR WAY TO GOD'S EYE VIEW

John the apostle wept when he first witnessed heaven's drama, but John wouldn't weep now. *He received a backstage pass, and now he knows the beginning from the end. His eyes are upon the Solution and not the problem; now he is a worshiper, not a wailer.* (p. 167)

hope you understand that none of this would work if God weren't truly God. If He were anything less than He really is, then virtually everything He says in His Book (and *absolutely everything* I say in my much less important books) would be false advertising. Yet it is true because He is true. He lifts us up when we magnify Him through our praise and worship.

WHAT DO YOU THINK?

Two brokenhearted sisters wept and grieved over hopes and dreams lost to the grave. From the perspective of Mary and Martha, their beloved Lazarus was dead and gone.[1] Jesus also wept at Lazarus's grave, but from His perspective

Lazarus was alive and well, simply awaiting the command to rise again.[2] He didn't say, "I *will be* the resurrection and the life." He said, "I *am* the resurrection and the life."[3] (p. 158)

How do you view the promises of God in His Word? Do you unconsciously read them as "something for somebody else in some other place at some other time," or as God's promises made "to me, right now and right here"? Explain.

TAKE IT PERSONALLY!

Who experiences the gripping emotions of anxiousness, fear, or terror during a dramatic presentation? Not the players on the stage. They are sure of the outcome. That experience of anxiety is reserved for the audience because they don't know the plot in the script. (p. 160)

ERRONEOUS ASSUMPTIONS, PRESUMPTIONS, AND MISALIGNED PARADIGMS

Desperation took the stage as the apostle and the company of heaven scoured three realms for someone who was worthy to open the Book. John said they found no one in heaven (that is the dominion of God);

they found no one in the earth (that is the dominion of man); and no one was worthy under the earth (that is the dominion of the demonic).[4] . . .

John the apostle was experiencing human emotions not usually associated with the realm of heaven. Who would ever expect to hear someone crying in despair within sight of the throne of God Himself? This man was viewing heavenly beings of inestimable power, engulfed in the glory of God's crystal-floored throne room, yet his fear of the unknown outcome had overwhelmed him. (pp. 160–61)

We underestimate the negative effects of fear on the human soul. Fear finds its way into our lives, thinking patterns, behavior, and religious patterns in ways we often overlook. Describe the times you have personally felt a wave of fear or the sharp prick of worry interrupt your thoughts . . .

- In the middle of a worship service, after some totally irrelevant thought about taxes due, work deadlines, or some threatening situation encountered during the week pushed its way to the surface.

- As you were worshiping and praising God in your home or during a small group Bible study.

- Moments after you dropped your head on the pillow after a remarkable day in the presence of the Lord.

- In the middle of the night just before the morning when you were scheduled to preach, teach a Sunday school class, lead worship, make a major step of faith, or talk to a friend about the Lord.

REMEMBER THIS!

Behold, *the Lion of the tribe of Judah,* the Root of David, has prevailed to open the scroll and to loose its seven seals. (Rev. 5:5, emphasis added)

MORE ERRONEOUS ASSUMPTIONS, PRESUMPTIONS, AND MISALIGNED PARADIGMS

The heavenly elder said, "Behold, *the Lion,*" while the earthly elder and apostle said, "I looked . . . [there] stood *a Lamb.*" Is the Bible wrong? Was John's memory beginning to show the ravages of the years? Hardly. Even a casual examination of the book of Revelation demonstrates that John had an amazing ability to communicate exact detail and amazing mysteries with skill. (p. 163)

The following statements represent some of the widely varying opinions about this scripture passage circulating through the church at any given time.

Circle true or false for each statement:

1. T / F   This is only a literary device. We shouldn't make much of it.

2. T / F   John was an old man who was half asleep. We should give him a little grace and write off this apparent difference in what was seen.

3. T / F   This should serve as a warning to us that we only see things "in part." There is another side to every situation, a view that can only be seen from God's elevated perspective.

WHAT DO YOU THINK?

Can you imagine John saying, "I just looked in heaven and I didn't see a lion. So where are you pointing, sir?" "Behold, the Lion of the tribe of Judah." So John wiped the tears of trouble from his eyes, looked toward the throne, and saw a Lamb once again.

149

The problem isn't error; it is *perspective*. When John the Beloved looked upon the scene at that point in the Revelation, he saw the prophetic performance through the eyes and perspective of an audience member having no inside understanding of the divine script or sacred plot line. That is our problem too. We need divine help. We need to get a God's eye view on things. I suppose another way to describe it is to say *we need a backstage pass*. (p. 163)

1. In your opinion, do you really need divine perspective in your life or does this idea really seem silly to you? Explain.

2. Have you ever experienced the pressure of the unknown making a difficult situation impossible, and then felt the pressure release when fresh information and knowledge took away your fear and anxiety? Describe it.

2. Did your personal experience help you understand this concept of "worshiping your way to God's eye view"? Explain.

TAKE IT PERSONALLY!

Have you recently said to yourself, "I'm not going to be able to make it . . . I can't make my marriage work. No matter what I do, I run out of money long before I run out of month"? If you are a child of God but you still feel hopeless, helpless, and trapped much of the time, *God has a backstage pass for you!* (p. 164)

MORE ERRONEOUS ASSUMPTIONS, PRESUMPTIONS, AND MISALIGNED PARADIGMS

Again, I have good news for you. God has a backstage pass for you, and it is heaven's authorization to privileged access, the key to help you understand the mysteries of God. *That backstage pass is called worship.*

Did you notice an interesting perspective in the exchange between the celestial being in heaven and the apostle from earth? I couldn't help noticing that the one who was wailing had his eyes on the problem, and the one who was worshiping had his eyes on the

Solution. Worship has a direct effect upon your perspective of heavenly things. (p. 165)

When things go wrong in life, the flesh instinctively moves us toward anger, fear, or uncontrollable sorrow. If we fail to rein in the flesh and walk in the Spirit:

1. T / F   It doesn't really matter because I am powerless to change my future.

2. T / F   Our eyes remain on the problem instead of upon the Solution.

3. T / F   We will "wail" when we should be worshiping God.

4. T / F   We will be stuck with a low perspective instead of God's eye view.

WHAT DO YOU THINK?

God says, "I'm going to give you a backstage pass. This will allow you to worship your way to a higher perspective. It will help you get a God's eye view of things in heaven and on earth so you can perceive things just as the heavenly beings and elders do."

When your worship takes you high enough to gain a God's eye view of the celestial drama called the mystery of God, you will see that the One opening the scrolls is not just a scarred Lamb in weakness; He is also the Lion of Judah released in unmatched strength and power.

Paul described your special backstage seating assignment when he said

He *"raised us up together,* and made us *sit together in the heavenly places* in Christ Jesus."[5] (pp. 166–67)

1. Why isn't it "blasphemous" to believe we can and should see things from God's eye view in the heavenly places?

2. In your opinion, how is it possible for Jesus to be both a lion and a lamb at the same time?

3. How is it possible for you to be living here on earth while at the same time you see things from God's eye view, seated together with Him in heavenly places?

MORE ERRONEOUS ASSUMPTIONS, PRESUMPTIONS, AND MISALIGNED PARADIGMS

God will talk to you about things that Satan cannot figure out or understand. What Satan *does* have is an eyewitness memory of thousands of years of tortured human history and angelic rebellion to draw from. It is inevitable that anyone who could spend that much time studying the behavior patterns, innate weaknesses, and unredeemed appetites of human beings would develop an impressive bank of knowledge—but not *all* knowledge. (p. 168)

Many Christians would never admit it, but they think and live as if Satan knows all things and possesses nearly as much power as God Himself.

1. Explain why this isn't true.

2. Provide any examples you can think of to illustrate your answer (e.g., "Satan is just an angel but Jesus is the Son of God").

3. Explain how you think Satan uses the knowledge he's gained over centuries of watching human behavior to tempt, bully, or frighten people.

WHAT DO YOU THINK?

Jesus, the Son of God, the divine player on the stage of destiny, chose to stay "in character" in His body of human weakness until the Lamb died. We must understand that the Lamb on the cross and the Lamb the apostle John saw before the throne of God a half century after the events of Calvary are also the "Lamb slain from the foundation of the world!"[6] (p. 169)

1. What does this tell you about God and His relationship with time?

2. Does it offer any insights to the way God sees *you* and your future?

3. You are forced to look in three directions with mostly limited vision: the past, the present, and the future. What does the Bible mean when it says, God "sees the end from the beginning"?

FILLING THE VOID

When _____ is _____ and the ____ __ ___ falls prophetically on someone's life, Satan begins to get a _____ on _____. As I said before, *heel* bruises will make you limp, but *head* bruises can be fatal! When _____ _____ and the _____ _____, when _____ _____ begins to sink in, the _____ pronouncement, "You shall _____ on _____," becomes a _____ to God's children.

Hell's ____-___ alert sounds. Demons run for "____" _____ away from the uplifted "heels" of _____ _____. Satan knew that God had a strange _____ for the creatures descended from _____ and ___, and that the _____ One liked to use them as _____ and _____ in the _____ realm. (pp. 170–71)

WHAT DO YOU THINK?

Why is it that every time Satan senses the rising tide of anointing he goes after the babies? Perhaps he illogically feels it's better to kill them before they prophetically mature. If that is true, we are living in a generation that has seen infanticide numerically go through the roof.

About the only difference between abortion and Satan's wholesale slaughter of infants in the time of Moses or Jesus' birth is technology. Lucifer now has the technology to kill an infant in the mother's womb. I think that reveals his level of fear—he senses revival coming. If Satan *fears* the anointing on the future of a generation, how much should we *believe* in the anointing on the upcoming generations? (pp. 171–72)

1. Do you believe there is a great anointing on the younger generations, or have you written them off as unsalvageable? Why?

2. If the "Me" generation promoted abortion to the level of a nationally recognized industry, what might be accomplished by a supernatural

"Him" generation composed of members from every nation, tribe, tongue, and age-group?

MORE ERRONEOUS ASSUMPTIONS, PRESUMPTIONS, AND MISALIGNED PARADIGMS

The Scriptures sum up Satan's celestial goof in just one phrase: *"Had they known,* they would not have crucified the Lord of glory."[7] What Satan didn't know has been revealed to you and me! It unlocks the key to your future!

Think about this: Jesus said He possesses the keys of hell and death.[8] If Satan doesn't even have the keys to his own house, how can he lock you up? How can Lucifer keep you in prison when Jesus said, "The gates of hell will not prevail"? *I feel a jail break spirit coming on!* You just got a backstage pass to the drama of redemption and found out it is a "Get Out of Jail Free" card! (p. 174)

1. What happened to the picture of Satan in your mind when you read that he doesn't even have the keys to his own house? (The truth of

God's Word about the power of God's Son will always put the adversary back in his place!)

2. Do you feel a "jail break spirit" coming on in your life and in the lives of those you love? Why?

3. How will you release a "jail break spirit" into the lives of other people around you?

REMEMBER THIS!

Make no mistake. That baby is not just a baby. He is the Ancient of Days who will stand to take possession and rule the whole earth. (p. 176)

WHAT DO YOU THINK?

Can you describe what a dragon looks like? If you assemble a list of its distinguishing features according to human folklore, it would include big teeth, massive size, scaly armored skin, clawed paws, a deadly lashing tail, leathery wings, and the ability to bellow streams of fire and great clouds of black smoke.

The funny thing about dragons is that they don't really exist . . .

The truth is that the dragon of mythology consists of all of our greatest fears wrapped up into one. It is every bad dream about large carnivorous teeth, imposing size, fire and smoke, scales, and ripping claws wrapped up into one imaginary nightmare.

. . . It is true that Satan once wielded a measure of power on the earth, but a Lion from heaven destroyed his stronghold, took his keys, stole all of his goods, and deflated his "red dragon balloon."[9]

What do we have left to fear? A dragon with diminished size, no teeth, no claws, and no fire . . . is just a lizard. I'm sorry but the dragon is gone— all you have left is an old, wrinkled lizard. Now we're getting somewhere. So things are not as they seem from man's point of view once you see them from God's eye view. (pp. 176–78)

1. Describe why you will never "look" at Satan in the same way again.

2. Think of traumatic past events in your life and describe how you would handle things differently today in the light of what you know about the Lion and the wrinkled lizard.

3. What is the key to seeing things differently in life as Christians?

REMEMBER THIS!

Worship puts Satan in his place, and it puts God in His place! (p. 178)

MORE ERRONEOUS ASSUMPTIONS, PRESUMPTIONS, AND MISALIGNED PARADIGMS

If you will spread your wings of worship, you won't need the reassuring whispers of celestial elders to tell you that everything is going to be all right. Worship Him. You are wearing the robe of a priest and the crown of a king—it's true. Take it from John the apostle who wrote,

> To Him who loved us and washed us from our sins in His own blood, and *has made us kings and priests to His God and Father.*[10]

God doesn't want you *down* looking *up*. He wants you *up* looking *down*. (pp. 178–79)

1. Do you read God's Word and believe it as true and applicable to *your* life, or do you study it as you would a book on philosophy, history, or sociology? (Be honest—support your answer with examples from your life. The point of this isn't to justify our past performance but to influence future performance.)

2. When the Bible says He "has made us kings and priests," is that in the future tense (describing a future action), or the past tense (describing something He has already completed)? Explain.

3. What does it mean for us right now? Does it inspire you to change your paradigm and alter your perspective?

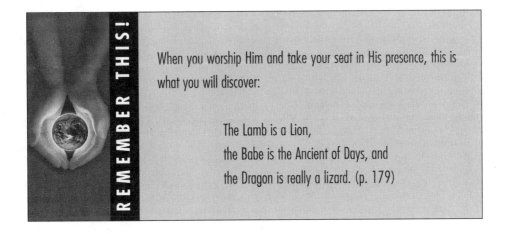

REMEMBER THIS!

When you worship Him and take your seat in His presence, this is what you will discover:

The Lamb is a Lion,
the Babe is the Ancient of Days, and
the Dragon is really a lizard. (p. 179)

WHAT DO YOU THINK?

Once worship takes you high enough and close enough to His presence, the lie dies and the truth comes to light. If I can get you to spread your wings of worship, you will gain privileged access to the heavenly script and discover the truth for yourself. I'm trying to unveil the Lion of Judah, exalt the Lamb of God, and unmask the dragon . . .

The perspective of worship changes everything about the way you see God in His glory and Satan in his fall. It's time to look at the red dragon again from a God's eye view.

Satan has a recurring nightmare about a shriveled and weakened lizard tied to a chain held by a powerful archangel. If that isn't bad enough, he keeps seeing flashes of a huge Lion's paw playfully batting the cowering lizard back and forth on God's front porch from time to time. (p. 180)

1. Describe ways and areas in which "the lie must die" about Satan's supposed power in the heavens and the earth.[11]

2. What do you intend to do to "gain privileged access to the heavenly script"?

3. How will your life "unveil the Lion of Judah, exalt the Lamb of God, and unmask the dragon"? Is this really possible?

NOTES

NOTES

10

COSTUMED CHARACTERS

THE LAMB IS A LION, THE BABE IS THE ANCIENT OF DAYS, THE DRAGON IS A LIZARD

We've had a peek at the full dress rehearsal for the grand finale; we've seen the end from the beginning. Somehow, some way, we must begin to live life on God's "high" way instead of fearing death on Satan's low way.

There is a high way built especially for us. No amount of money will put you there, but a simple surrender of all that you are entitles you to literally live there if you dare. (pp. 185–86)

It all seems too good to be true, but it is true nevertheless. It also seems too outlandish and altogether "supernatural" to be true, but it is nevertheless. In the end, it seems too right to dismiss and too logical to disregard, but many of us do it nonetheless.

The words quoted above from *God's Eye View* make sense to you because you embrace the truth about the Lamb who is a Lion and the Babe who is the Ancient of Days. You just want to know how to see things His way.

169

WHAT DO YOU THINK?

Do you remember reading somewhere that God sees all things "from the end to the beginning"? Now that God has given us a backstage pass to sit with Him in the heavenlies, we can enjoy a God's eye view of events past, present, and future. Obviously we still won't see and know all things as He does, but having the privilege of peeking into the way things really are should significantly change the way we act and live today and tomorrow.

We shouldn't be flinching like other people do when the antagonist of our race makes an attack on us. We've read the back of the book; we've seen the final act, and we know who wins. (p. 182)

1. How will "having a backstage pass" affect your day-to-day routines and responses to crises?

2. Will it totally eliminate all problems, or will it simply help you endure and overcome them in most cases? How?

3. Will the "backstage pass" of God's eye view cause you to feel more independent of God or even more dependent and even more amazed at His power and wisdom? Why?

ERRONEOUS ASSUMPTIONS, PRESUMPTIONS, AND MISALIGNED PARADIGMS

I was looking forward to capturing a treasure of those little smiles that you hold forever in the memory bank of your mind when her face took on a look of sheer terror. Just as we went through the front gate, a big seven-foot blue TV character bounced over to shake my daughter's hand. She climbed me like I was a tree.

The person in the costume quickly grasped the problem and silently moved on, but the daddy in me just knew that the rest of the day had been put on hold. Every time my little girl saw some oversized character in the park, she was going to be paranoid. That meant that I had to do something. (pp. 182–83)

1. Is there an area in your life—whether or not you are a "little person"—in which an early fright or wound "put your life on hold"? If so, explain.

2. Are you ready for your Father to "do something" about the problem that haunts your life and limits your ability to fulfill your destiny in Christ? If so, what do you want Him to do?

3. Is there an area in your own children's lives in which you must do something to help them win freedom once again? If so, explain.

FILLING THE VOID

Given the choice between seeing you _____ in _____ _____ or _____
_____, the devil will _____ _____ sheer _____ for you. What Satan
doesn't want is for you to _____ your heavenly _____'_ _____ and whisper
reassuringly, "_ _____, _____—it's _____ a _____."
_____ and _____ _____ are the devil's stock-in-trade.
Deprived of all true _____ by the _____ who is a Lion, the _____
and wizard of _____ and terror devotes his miserable existence to _____ and
_____ the people of God (he doesn't really have to worry very much about
___ _____—they _____ _____ to him anyway). (pp. 184–85)

TAKE IT
PERSONALLY!

Things should be different now. You've had a good peek through the mesh on Satan's lumpy dragon costume—the one without any teeth. You have God's backstage pass in your heart because you are a God Chasing worshiper, so you know how the cosmic drama ends. It's time to beat the devil with the fear stick now. (p. 185)

WHAT DO YOU THINK?

My father once wrote:

> *The Church is meant to be the devil's purgatory.* We can torment him while he is still on earth, but first we have to stop looking and living like we belong to him and stop running with his crowd.

Frankly, the wrong group is worried today. The Church shouldn't be worried about the enemy; he should be worried about us! The only reason he isn't very worried is because generally, we are too tame, domesticated, self-centered, and satisfied with mediocrity to be harmful to his health. (God calls it being "lukewarm.") (p. 185)

1. In what ways do Christians (and the church) look and live as if they belong with the world and its dark master? Are there reasons for this?

2. How may we "torment" the devil and create an ongoing "Purgatory" for him during our time on earth?

3. If we are "too tame, domesticated, self-centered, and satisfied with mediocrity" to worry him, what must happen to change us and how must we change to be "dangerous" to Satan and his fallen kingdom?

MORE ERRONEOUS ASSUMPTIONS, PRESUMPTIONS, AND MISALIGNED PARADIGMS

This high way isn't so much a track of gravel, asphalt, or reinforced concrete stretching from point A to point B. It is really a path of intimacy in Him. It is a place the ravenous beasts of the netherworld can never reach. Satan himself cannot touch you there, for it is a holy place. In fact, I am convinced this holy high way is really a person, the One who dared to claim the name "The Way." (p. 186)

Many people have a problem with scriptural phrases because they see everything as "black and white."

1. If Jesus did not really mean He was a garden path, gravel road, or physical highway composed of concrete or asphalt and stone when He called Himself "the Way," then what *did* He mean?

2. In your opinion, why do people find it easier to reach for a formula or program than to reach out to God?

3. What about you? Do you prefer the "chase" and passionate pursuit of His presence, or do you prefer a program or formula that promises to solve all of your problems? Why?

FILLING THE VOID

Although _____ paid the total _____ for our _____ with His life and His blood, __ must pay the price for _____ with _____ by laying down *our lives* _____. As far as I can tell, Jesus _____ intended for Christian _____ to begin and end the ____ ___ we kneel at an altar or _____ _____ in a meeting. I heard He wasn't really very ____-_____ about it. He told the folks at First Church of Jerusalem, "If anyone desires to ____ _____ Me, let him ____ himself, and take up his _____ daily, and _____ __."[1] (p. 188)

WHAT DO YOU THINK?

This kind of commitment and heavenly viewpoint may even take you to the point of literal death in certain instances.[2] It is difficult to sustain that level of commitment on a steady diet of religious platitudes, half-baked sermons from the previous decade, and a few hours of prime-time Christian television. Sometimes you need to make a greater personal sacrifice to achieve a God's eye view of His purposes and receive a greater deposit of His presence. (p. 188)

1. Athletics has changed dramatically over the last one hundred years. It was normal for athletes in earlier years to smoke, drink heavily, eat poorly, and begin an athletic contest without warming up or preparing in any way. Experts now strongly discourage all of these

practices. Why do we consider these behaviors among athletes so dangerous today?

2. Do you believe you can maintain or achieve a victorious Christian life while feeding your soul religious platitudes, half-baked sermons, and a good dose of prime-time Christian television? Why or why not?

3. Why should commitment and a heavenly viewpoint be connected in the minds of genuine God Chasers? (Can you think of a Scripture that supports or establishes this connection?)

MORE ERRONEOUS ASSUMPTIONS, PRESUMPTIONS, AND MISALIGNED PARADIGMS

Some forms of worship have a greater spiritual magnitude or "volume," but it is all worship. If you compared the "volume" of my boyish sacrifice of a Heath bar with that of a forty-day fast, one would be a whisper and the other one a shout. Yet they have the same quality, and both come from the same source. (p. 190)

How many potential Ludwig Beethovens, Abraham Lincolns, or Billy Grahams fell by the wayside over the centuries because they feared taking the first imperfect and potentially risky step toward greater things?

1. Describe ways you failed to do anything in a situation because you feared doing something wrong, imperfectly, or incorrect in your initial effort.

2. Did you compare yourself to someone else who was proficient in that activity? If so, explain.

REMEMBER THIS!

Once you say yes to God and begin to put the pursuit of His presence above the pursuit of His presents, something begins to change in you. You hunger for something different! (p. 191)

WHAT DO YOU THINK?

There is a chance you may return to those old pursuits for a bout of temporary self-indulgence on the curb of life, but you will find they've lost their power to satisfy (and just might make you as sick as a dog). There is a reason for it all—God is raising up a worshiping, working, wartime church as opposed to a passive and somewhat self-absorbed peacetime church. (p. 191)

1. Describe the differences you might find between "a worshiping, working wartime church" and "a passive and somewhat self-absorbed peacetime church."

2. What about your church? Into which category does it generally fit?

MORE ERRONEOUS ASSUMPTIONS, PRESUMPTIONS, AND MISALIGNED PARADIGMS

To mix metaphors, God is trying to prepare us for a net-breaking harvest of disciples, and He will not tend to be lenient toward any church congregation that squanders through incompetence or laziness that portion of His harvest allotted to it. We are about to enter the season when the plowman will overtake the reaper. God has placed the church on an accelerated schedule. (p. 191)

1. Would your local church know what to do with a "net-breaking harvest of disciples" if genuine revival suddenly descended on your area? Why?

2. Do you believe God is "lenient" or "not lenient" with local church congregations, or are you convinced He doesn't care what local churches do or don't do? (Hint: If you want to know God's eye view perspective, read Revelation 2.)

WHAT DO YOU THINK?

Even God needs cooperation to make the harvest come in, and you have to do your part. The Lord has already done His part. Jesus meant what He said when He declared from the tree of Golgotha, "It is finished!"[3] If God has done His part, then that means the problem lies elsewhere. Whether we like it or not, *we* are the *weakest link* in God's lifeline to the world . . .

We are more bland than salty. Our light output resembles a 5-watt nightlight more than a 20,000-watt searchlight. We've invested more work and money to raising our comfort levels than to reaching out to the lost and hurting.

We closely resemble the tree that needed some fertilization and root work for a last chance. (pp. 192–93)

1. Is this passage from *God's Eye View* unfair and judgmental, or is it bluntly accurate? Why?

2. Why are we (the church and Christ's followers) "the *weakest link* in God's lifeline to the world"? How can we correct the problem?

TAKE IT
PERSONALLY!

Worship is *not* limited to church services inside the four walls of a church building where people gather around an altar or stage steps to cry and weep before the Lord. That is definitely an important part of it, but in this season worship begins the moment you say yes to every task, service, project, or activity instigated by God's Word and the Holy Spirit. (p. 193)

WHAT DO YOU THINK?

We've worshiped just about everything else *but* God, and we've done just about everything except what He asked us to do. Unfortunately we've paid a dear price for our lukewarm religiosity. All that is about to change. I can almost hear Grandfather Caughron shouting from the ramparts of heaven, "Hey, we're going to have some fasting around here!" Paul the apostle is at his side shouting to us, "Run the good race. Run to win. Never run merely to make a showing. Run for the prize." It's time to get serious. *Satan's ploys are God's toys.* (p. 194)

1. Imagine what would happen in your church and home if someone suddenly sensed the anointed of God and shouted, "Hey, we're going to have some fasting around here!" and "Run the good race. Run to win!" Describe some of the changes that might take place.

2. Are you ready to shout the announcement? Why?

MORE ERRONEOUS ASSUMPTIONS, PRESUMPTIONS, AND MISALIGNED PARADIGMS

The devil has lost his position, he's lost his place, he's lost his understanding, he's desperate, and he plots, "I've got to kill this anointing before it matures." Satan is a dream stealer. He wants to kill your dreams before they can come to maturity.

He's afraid of what you can do. As soon as you begin to dream, his ploy is to send somebody to say, "That will never happen." In every way possible he will try to abort the destiny God has woven into your life.

The enemy also wants to kill or divert your children before they step into the fullness of their destiny. No generation has been targeted for death and disintegration of identity on such a staggering scale as *this* generation of young people. (p. 194)

1. Are you "comfortable" with the above descriptions of such an intensely personal enemy as Satan, or do you prefer to believe in a nameless and essentially distant evil who doesn't seem to know your name and address?

2. Are these descriptions biblical in nature and tone, or do you see a more amiable and less threatening adversary in the Scriptures?

3. What are you prepared to do about this enemy of your dreams, destiny, and the future of your children?

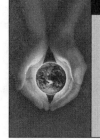

REMEMBER THIS!

We need God's eye view in every area of life. We've limped along with hampered vision long enough. (p. 194)

WHAT DO YOU THINK?

A God's eye view totally changes our day-to-day lives from the inside out. The Moravians were known as the "happy people" in an era when being happy was almost considered to be sinful. Why were they so happy? They had tapped into the wellspring of jubilant worship and exuberant praise. Their joy spilled over into the lives of the Wesley brothers and many other influential church leaders. (p. 195)

If your neighbors or unsaved friends were to describe your church using your life as a "spiritual thermometer," choose the most likely descriptive phrase and explain your choice below:

❏ The First Church of the Frozen Chosen

❏ The Friendly What's-Their-Names Church "all we know about them is they're out at noon every Sunday"

❏ The Local Granola Congregation (comprised of an assortment of fruits, flakes, and nuts in a box)

❏ The Sad, Somber Fellowship of the Hopeless Pilgrims (holding on desperately until it's all over)

❏ The Happy People Who Sometimes Don't Even Bother to Go Home

MORE ERRONEOUS ASSUMPTIONS, PRESUMPTIONS, AND MISALIGNED PARADIGMS

It has been said that some of the Christians who died as martyrs in Rome's Coliseum left this life singing hymns of joy to God. They had a God's eye view of a situation that seemed hopeless at the ground level of life without God. (p. 195)

TAKE IT
PERSONALLY!

I don't have to step on any theological or eschatological toes to declare the grand finale of our existence boils down to one word—*worship*. It is God's backstage pass to a whole new realm of vision, power, and authority rooted in intimacy with Him. It isn't complicated. Just take your cue from a little child in a crowded elevator:

"Pick me up, Daddy! I can't see from down here." (p. 195)

NOTES

NOTES

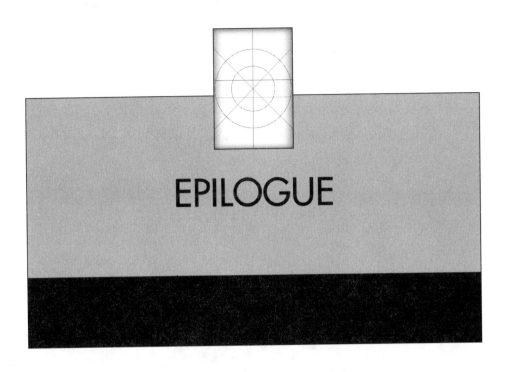

EPILOGUE

*May these ten way points assist you on the way to your final destination
of the heavenly Mount Moriah where, as a tourist from time, you will get
to view the eternal scene from God's eye view.* (p. 196)

I wrote the Epilogue to *God's Eye View* to help summarize the most important points I received from the Holy Spirit on this subject, and to help
them become a "change agent" in your life so that *you* can become a godly
change agent in the world around you!

I encourage you to read each "way point" on the "Glory Positioning
System" (GPS) and seek God's wisdom on what they mean and what you are
to do about them personally. Invest the time to write in your answers. They
will serve as key "way markers" for your life and personal pursuit of God and
His kingdom.

1. We can't always see clearly from down here. It's time to admit our
   sight problem and ask Daddy for help. The disciples humbly asked

Jesus to teach them how to pray. We need to throw our hands in the air and humbly ask with childlike hearts, "Pick me up, Daddy. I can't see from down here." (p. 196)

WHAT DO YOU THINK?

(In your own words . . .)

WHAT WILL YOU DO ABOUT IT?

(In your own life and the lives of those you touch . . .)

2. We usually think zero is bad, but in God's eye view it is His favorite number for building His relationships with us (because zero is His favorite starting place for miracles). We must rediscover the virtue of zero and look to Him as our Rock and strength for what we face today and tomorrow. (pp. 196–97)

WHAT DO YOU THINK?

(In your own words . . .)

WHAT WILL YOU DO ABOUT IT?

(In your own life and the lives of those you touch . . .)

3. Passion must return to the church so Presence can come to stay. We've put up with the antics of self-appointed passion police far too long. Either we chase God, or we pursue the approval of fickle flesh (I know which one I would choose). God is tearing down every "No P.D.A." sign in His church—He comes for our passion, not for our religious pomp and circumstance. (p. 197)

WHAT DO YOU THINK?

(In your own words . . .)

WHAT WILL YOU DO ABOUT IT?

(In your own life and the lives of those you touch . . .)

4. We must rediscover the biblical power of position. Sons and daughters don't have to shout out their petitions from the front porch. We can sashay into His presence as children of the house and approach Him as beloved family members. (p. 197)

WHAT DO YOU THINK?

(In your own words . . .)

WHAT WILL YOU DO ABOUT IT?

(In your own life and the lives of those you touch . . .)

5. A heavenly perspective puts Satan the accuser in his rightful place—
outside in the cold. While the tattler and his tattletales are stuck
outside on the porch, we get to enjoy the privileged access of
chosen sons and daughters in our Daddy's presence. (p. 197)

WHAT DO YOU THINK?

(In your own words . . .)

WHAT WILL YOU DO ABOUT IT?

(In your own life and the lives of those you touch . . .)

6. Stop turning the molehills of passing distress under your feet into mountains that may ultimately threaten your destiny. Rediscover the proper use and potential of the power of magnification. "Come magnify the Lord with me—in *our* sight and in the eyes of the world." (p. 197)

WHAT DO YOU THINK?

(In your own words . . .)

WHAT WILL YOU DO ABOUT IT?

(In your own life and the lives of those you touch . . .)

7. There has been a thief in the house. Someone took our worship and left a cheap counterfeit in its place. Just as the enemies of Israel ransacked the temple of Solomon of all of its pure gold implements of worship, someone managed to steal pure worship from the church. We've replaced it with a cheap substitute covered with the shiny veneer of religious tradition and empty ritual (and charismatics, pentecostals, and evangelicals have just as many religious traditions and empty rituals as their high church brethren). God doesn't care what the nameplate says on the front of your building—He wants to know if He will find "true worship in spirit and in truth" in your heart. (pp. 197–98)

WHAT DO YOU THINK?

(In your own words . . .)

WHAT WILL YOU DO ABOUT IT?

(In your own life and the lives of those you touch . . .)

8. It's time to stop shouting at the devil on the porch and start whispering to Daddy in the kitchen. We will accomplish more warfare through worship than through every other means available to us. Frankly we should probably use every tool God provides to us, but above all we are called to worship Him. God fought Israel's most important battles *for them*. (p. 198)

WHAT DO YOU THINK?

(In your own words . . .)

WHAT WILL YOU DO ABOUT IT?

(In your own life and the lives of those you touch . . .)

9. God has given us a backstage pass with all of the rights and privileges of heavenly citizens positioned around His throne. He expects and anticipates our immediate arrival to take our seats with Him for a God's eye view of the cosmic drama going on *right now*. The exclusive pass is in your heart and on your lips even now— worship Him, and be transported to a higher point of view. (p. 198)

WHAT DO YOU THINK?

(In your own words . . .)

WHAT WILL YOU DO ABOUT IT?

(In your own life and the lives of those you touch . . .)

10. Take on a new view of our brief earthly lives by allowing Him to project them over the greater canvas of His eternal purposes. Acquire a new view from His side, revealing the end to the beginning. It will totally change the way we live each day and make the most of each moment. (p. 198)

WHAT DO YOU THINK?

(In your own words . . .)

WHAT WILL YOU DO ABOUT IT?

(In your own life and the lives of those you touch . . .)

NOTES

GODChasers.network

GodChasers.network is the ministry of Tommy and Jeannie Tenney. Their heart's desire is to see the presence and power of God fall—not just in churches, but on cities and communities all over the world.

How to contact us:

By Mail:

GodChasers.network
P.O. Box 3355
Pineville, Louisiana 71361
USA

By Phone:

Voice: 318.44CHASE (318.442.4273)
Fax: 318.442.6884
Orders: 888.433.3355

By Internet:

E-mail: GodChaser@GodChasers.net
Website: www.GodChasers.net

Join Today

When you join the **GodChasers.network** we'll send you a free teaching tape!

If you share in our vision and want to stay current on how the Lord is using GodChasers.network, please add your name to our mailing list. We'd like to keep you updated on what the Spirit is saying through Tommy. We'll also send schedule updates and make you aware of new resources as they become available.

Sign up by calling or writing to:

Tommy Tenney
GodChasers.network
P.O. Box 3355
Pineville, Louisiana 71361-3355
USA

318-44CHASE (318.442.4273)
or sign up online at http://www.GodChasers.net/lists/

We regret that we are only able to send regular postal mailings to certain countries at this time. If you live outside the U.S. you can still add your postal address to our mailing list—you will automatically begin to receive our mailings as soon as they are available in your area.

E-mail Announcement List

If you'd like to receive information from us via e-mail, just provide an e-mail address when you contact us and let us know that you want to be included on the e-mail announcement list!

Run With Us!

Become a GodChasers.network Monthly Revival Partner

GodChasers are people whose hunger for Him compels them to run—not walk—towards a deeper and more meaningful relationship with the Almighty! For them, it isn't just a casual pursuit. Traditional Sundays and Wednesdays aren't enough—they need Him everyday, in every situation and circumstance, the good times and bad. Are you a GodChaser? Do you believe the body of Christ needs Revival? If my mandate of personal, National and International Revival is a message that resonates in your spirit, I want you to prayfully consider Running with us! Our Revival Partners fuel GodChasers.network to bring the message of unity and the pursuit of His presence around the world! And the results are incredible, yet humbling. As a Revival Partner, your monthly seed becomes the matches we use to set Revival fires around the globe.

For your monthly support of at least thirty dollars or more, I will send you free, personal fuel each month. This could be audio or videotapes of what I feel the Lord is saying that month. In addition, you will receive discounts on all of our ministry resources. Your Revival Partner status will automatically include you in invitation-only gatherings where I will minister in a more intimate setting.

I rely on our Revival Partners to intercede for the ministry in prayer and even minister with us at GodChaser gatherings around the country. I love to sow seed in peoples' lives and have learned that you can't out give God, He always multiplies the seed! If we give Him something to work with, there's no limit how many He can feed, or how many Revival fires can be started!

Will you run with us every month?

In Pursuit,

Tony Tony

Tommy Tenney

Become a Monthly Revival Partner by calling or writing to:

Tommy Tenney/GodChasers.network
P.O. Box 3355
Pineville, Louisiana 71361-3355
318.44CHASE (318.442.4273)

ABOUT THE AUTHOR

TOMMY TENNEY is the author of the bestselling series *The God Chasers, God's Favorite House, The God Catcher,* and *God's Eye View.* Adding to that series now are *How to Be a God Chaser and a Kid Chaser,* coauthored with his mother, and *Chasing God, Serving Man,* a revelatory revisiting of the story of Mary and Martha. He is also the author of another series of books on unity that includes *God's Dream Team, Answering God's Prayer,* and *God's Secret to Greatness.*

Tommy spent ten years pastoring and has spent over twenty years in itinerant ministry, traveling to more than forty nations. He speaks in over 150 venues each year sharing his heart with many thousands. His two passions are *The Presence of God* and *Unity in the Body of Christ.* To help others pursue these twin passions, he founded the GodChasers.network, a ministry organized to distribute his writing and speaking through various mediums. Tommy is a prolific author with more than one million books in print each year, and eight bestselling titles to date. His books have been translated into more than thirty languages.

Three generations of ministry in his family heritage have given Tommy a unique perspective on ministry. He has a gifting to lead hungry people into the presence of God. He and his wife, Jeannie, understand the value of intimacy with God and humility in serving God's people.

The Tenneys reside in Louisiana with their three daughters and two Yorkies.

NOTES

CHAPTER 1

    1. Isaiah 55:8.

    2. 1 Corinthians 2:16 NLT, emphasis added.

    3. Acts 2:1–41.

    4. Luke 9:23.

    5. Psalm 46:10.

    6. 2 Corinthians 5:15–17, emphasis added. My purpose is simple: we should all submit our thoughts, assumptions, presumptions, and paradigms to the Word of God and the Holy Spirit regularly. Life experiences have a way of forcing our rigid theology through the "reality grinder of truth." This keeps us true to the goal of becoming "more like Him" rather than "more like our dry and untested theoretical concepts of Him." The Old Testament portraits of the Messiah were true and accurate, but they provided only a brief and partial picture of the full reality of Jesus Christ, the Son of God come in the flesh. Most of the religious types in His day chose to cling to their faded two-dimensional snapshots of God rather than embrace the three-dimensional reality of *Emmanuel*, "God among us." God doesn't ask us to take "either one or the other." He wants

us to discover how the reality of His presence is totally compatible with the reality of God revealed in the Old Testament and the New.

CHAPTER 2

1. See Psalm 14:1; 53:1.

2. *Merriam Webster's Collegiate Dictionary,* 10th ed. (Springfield, MA: Merriam-Webster, 1994), p. 515.

3. I deal with this concept and with God's love and the compassionate response of Christian people to the devastation and tragedy experienced by the victims, rescuers, their families, and the American people on September 11, 2001, in my book *Trust and Tragedy: Encountering God in Times of Crisis* (Nashville, TN: Thomas Nelson Publishers, 2001).

4. See Matthew 19:17.

5. John 12:24.

CHAPTER 3

1. Matthew 22:37.

2. Joshua 24:15.

CHAPTER 4

1. 2 Corinthians 12:9.

2. See Isaiah 26:9.

3. The answer is "members."

CHAPTER 5

1. 1 John 2:1–2 NLT.

2. See 1 Peter 5:8; Revelation 12:10.

3. See John 8:44 NIV.

4. See Matthew 18:34–35. This statement is based upon what may be

Jesus' least popular parable due to its severe implications. One thing is beyond debate: God hates unforgiveness.

CHAPTER 6

1. See Isaiah 40:31, emphasis added.

2. James 1:6.

3. Psalm 34:3, emphasis added.

4. Luke 1:46–47, emphasis added.

5. Job 3:25.

6. speak good things; mouth speaks.

7. idle word; speak; account; judgment; your words; justified; your words; be condemned.

8. fruit of his mouth; produce of his lips; Death and life; power of the tongue.

9. refrain his tongue; evil; lips from speaking deceit.

10. the tongue is a fire; tongue; it defiles the whole body; sets on fire; it is set on fire.

11. tame the tongue; an unruly evil; deadly poison; we bless; we curse; same mouth.

12. Summarized in rearranged order from Numbers 13:31–33, emphasis added.

CHAPTER 7

1. Psalm 121:8, emphasis added.

2. Judges 15:18, emphasis added.

3. See Judges 15:17–19.

4. See 1 Peter 5:6–7.

CHAPTER 8

1. See Romans 2:11 KJV.

2. Isaiah 40:22.

3. Psalm 24:3–4, emphasis added.

4. Luke 9:23.

5. 2 Timothy 3:12.

6. James 2:18.

7. Romans 12:1, emphasis added.

CHAPTER 9

1. See John 11:32–35.

2. See John 11:14–44.

3. John 11:25, emphasis added.

4. See Revelation 5:3.

5. Ephesians 2:6, emphasis added.

6. Revelation 13:8.

7. 1 Corinthians 2:8, emphasis added.

8. See Revelation 1:18.

9. John depicted Satan as a fiery red dragon (Rev. 12:3).

10. Revelation 1:6, emphasis added.

11. You should realize that these descriptions of Satan's diminished importance and shriveled abilities are valid *only* for those whose eyes are on the Lamb and Lion of God. The lie dies *as the truth comes to light*. Remember that you magnify whatever fills your vision—keep your eyes on the King of kings, not the fallen angel of light.

CHAPTER 10

1. See Luke 9:23.

2. See Revelation 12:11.

3. John 19:30.

BOOKS BY

Tony Tony

THE GOD CHASERS
$12.00 plus $4.50 S&H

What is a God Chaser? A person whose hunger exceeds his reach...a person whose passion for God's presence presses him to chase the impossible in hopes that the uncatchable might catch him.

The great GodChasers of the Scripture—Moses, Daniel, David—see how they were driven by hunger born of tasting His goodness. They had seen the invisible and nothing else satisfied. Add your name to the list. Come join the ranks of the God Chasers.

GOD'S EYE VIEW
$23.00 plus $4.50 S&H

In this simple but powerful book, worship will teach you "throne zone" secrets. The higher you go in worship, the bigger God appears (and the smaller your problems seem). If you can't see that from where you are presently sitting, there is a better seat available. The angels will usher you to your reserved seat in "heavenly places" and you will have *God's Eye View.*

CHASING GOD, SERVING MAN
$17.00 plus $4.50 S&H

Using the backdrop of Bethany and the house of Mary and Martha, Tommy Tenney biblically explores new territory. The revolutionary concepts in this book can change your life. You will discover who you really are (and unlock the secret of who "they" really are)!

MARY'S PRAYERS & MARTHA'S RECIPES
$18.00 plus $4.50 S&H

There are a lot of prayer books and many great spiritual books but there are precious few prayer and compassion books that are practical workbooks as well. Mary's Prayers and Martha's Recipes will be your own special resource for both seasons in your life.

We must learn to work like Martha and worship like Mary. It is essential that we do not do one to the exclusion of the other. It takes the loving service of Martha and the adoring prayers of Mary to complete the full ministry of the Body of Christ in this world.

GodChasers.network
P.O. Box 3355, Pineville, Louisiana 71361-3355
318-44CHASE (318.442.4273)

VIDEOTAPE ALBUMS BY

Tommy Tenney

FOLLOW THE MAN ON THE COLT
Video $20.00 plus $4.50 S&H

From humility to authority.... If we learn to ride the colt of humility, then we qualify to ride on the stallion of authority.

(This new video helps us understand that we all start this journey crawling—which strengththens us to walk—that empowers us to run—and rewards us to ride!) Enjoy this great teaching by Tommy Tenney on following the Man on the colt. It will change the way you see the obstacles put in your path! Remember, there is never a testimony without a test!

BROWNSVILLE WILDFIRE SERIES, VOL. 1
"Born to Be a Worshiper"
Video $20.00 plus $4.50 S&H

God would rather hear the passionate praises of His children than the perfection of heavenly worship. It isn't about how good we are as singers, or how skilled we are as musicians. It isn't about singing catchy choruses with clever words. It's all about GOD, and if we'll let our guard down and allow ourselves to truly worship Him, we'll find that He's closer than we ever imagined. If you've been born into God's kingdom, then you were born to be a worshiper! It's time to do the very thing that we were created for!

TURNING ON THE LIGHT OF THE GLORY
Video $20.00 plus $4.50 S&H

Tommy deals with turning on the light of the glory and presence of God, and he walks us through the necessary process and ingredients to potentially unleash what His Body has always dreamed of.

GOING HOME FROM A FUNERAL
Video ~~$20.00~~ $10.00 plus $4.50 S&H

Our country is now in a crisis. Some things will never be the same. Our national mentality is as if we are "going home from a funeral." We are no longer in the orderly, controlled funeral procession. Cars have scattered, taking their own routes back to individual homes and routines. The lights are off and reality hits.

GodChasers.network
P.O. Box 3355, Pineville, Louisiana 71361-3355
318-44CHASE (318.442.4273)
www.GodChasers.net

God's Eye View

In *God's Eye View*, Tommy Tenney explores how worship lifts us up to see the trouble we face from God's perspective instead of being trapped in an earthly, time-bound viewpoint. The higher we go, the smaller our problems seem. Tenney also teaches the Principle of Magnification: The closer you get to something, the bigger it appears. In other words, worship not only "shrinks" our problems; it also magnifies God in our lives and to others.

Worship doesn't really change our problems; it just minimizes their influence over us as we focus on God. He doesn't promise to remove all of our circumstances, but God does assure us that in His presence and from His perspective—we can see things as they really are and not how they appear to be.

Higher than a bird's eye view, higher than a man's eye view is God's eye view.

ISBN 0-7852-6560-0

Catch Him!

 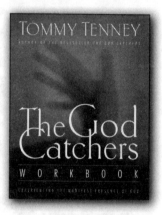 

The God
Catchers
ISBN 0-7852-6710-7

The God Catchers
Workbook
ISBN 0-7852-6623-2

Experiencing His
Presence
ISBN 0-7852-6619-4

Why do some believers experience genuine, life-changing, personal revival while others don't? In *The God Catchers* and its companions, *The God Catchers Workbook* and the devotional *Experiencing His Presence,* Tommy explains the difference: "God in a sense plays hide and seek. But like a loving parent, He always makes sure He can be found by those who take the time to look." Simply put, those who earnestly seek God rather than wait for something to happen find Him. Full of biblical and contemporary accounts of believers who chased God and caught Him, these three books will motivate readers to discover the joy of finding God and having a loving relationship with Him.

Look for all of these books at your local bookstore,
or by visiting the Web site www.ThomasNelson.com
or calling 1-800-441-0511.